Luke and the Pastoral Epistles

LUKE AND THE PASTORAL EPISTLES

Stephen G. Wilson

LONDON
SPCK

First published 1979
SPCK
Holy Trinity Church
Marylebone Road
London NW1 4DU

Printed in Great Britain by
R. & R. Clark Ltd., Edinburgh

ISBN 0 281 03676 4

To Jenny

Contents

Acknowledgement

Biblical quotations are from the Revised Standard Version of the Bible, copyrighted 1946, 1952, © 1971, 1973 by the Division of Christian Education of the National Council of the Churches of Christ in the U.S.A., and are used by permission.

Preface

It is my hope that readers will receive this book in the spirit with which it was written. In considering the evidence for connections between Luke–Acts and the Pastorals I have deliberately argued an extreme hypothesis, that of common authorship, in order to see what the evidence will bear. That there is a considerable amount of evidence, much of it overlooked, I have no doubt. That it is sufficient to support my hypothesis I consider to be an interesting possibility, and offer it to the reader as such.

There are many assumptions built into the argument. To argue for them all in detail would necessitate either frequent diversions in the main text or copious footnotes, neither of which seemed to me desirable. The footnotes, however, normally indicate where these points have been more fully discussed.

I am most grateful to Professor L. Gaston of Vancouver, Canada, and Professor C. K. Barrett of Durham, England, who read an early draft and encouraged me to complete and publish it. I would like to thank Carleton University who, through the office of the Dean of Arts, contributed towards the costs of preparation and publication. The book is dedicated to my wife.

Carleton University,   S. G. WILSON
Ottawa, 1977

Abbreviations

GENERAL

BC   Foakes-Jackson, F. J. and Lake, K., ed., *The Beginnings of Christianity*. London 1933.

BJRL   *Bulletin of the John Rylands Library*

BZ   *Biblische Zeitschrift*

CBQ   *Catholic Biblical Quarterly*

Ev. Th. *Evangelische Theologie*

JAC   *Jahrbuch für Antike und Christentum*

JBL   *Journal of Biblical Literature*

JTS   *Journal of Theological Studies*

NTS   *New Testament Studies*

RSV   Revised Standard Version

SBL   Society of Biblical Literature

SJT   *Scottish Journal of Theology*

SLA   Keck, L. E., and Martyn, J. L., ed., *Studies in Luke–Acts*. London 1968.

TDNT   *Theological Dictionary of the New Testament*

TLZ   *Theologische Literaturzeitung*

ZNW   *Zeitschrift für die neutestamentliche Wissenschaft*

FIRST-CENTURY AND PATRISTIC WRITINGS

Barn.	Epistle of Barnabas
Chrysostom, 2 *Tim. Hom.*	Chrysostom, *In II Timoth. Homiliae*
1 Clem.	First Epistle of Clement
2 Clem.	Second Epistle of Clement
Did.	*Didache*
Eusebius, *Hist. Eccl.*	Eusebius, *Historia Ecclesiastica*
Ign., *Eph.*	Ignatius, *Epistle to the Ephesians*
Iren., *Adv. Haer.*	Irenaeus, *Adversus Haereses*
Jerome, *De vir. illust.*	Jerome, *De viris illustribus*
Jos., *Ant.*	Josephus, *Antiquitates Iudaicae*
Jos., *War*	Josephus, *Bellum Judaicum*
Mart. Polyc.	*Martyrdom of Polycarp*
Philo, *Vit. Mos.*	Philo, *De Vita Mosis*
Philo, *In Flacc.*	Philo, *In Flaccum*
Philo, *Rer. div. Her.*	Philo, *Quis Rerum Divinarum Heres?*
Polybius, *Hist.*	Polybius, *Historiae*
Polyc., *Phil.*	Polycarp, *Epistle to the Philippians*
Tert., *Adv. Haer.*	Tertullian, *Adversus Haereses*

1
Introduction

The purpose of this essay is to defend the thesis that the author of
Luke–Acts also wrote the Pastoral Epistles. In an earlier study on
Luke–Acts, I argued that Luke was primarily motivated by
practical and pastoral concerns rather than theological issues.[1] It
often struck me then that the writings closest to Luke–Acts in the
New Testament were the Pastoral Epistles. A. T. Hanson says of
the author of the Pastorals (for the sake of brevity, henceforth
called the *Pastor*): 'He himself was not a man of original genius as
Paul was; indeed he cannot really be described as possessing a
theology or system of thought of his own. This is the last thing he
would have wanted. His great aim is not to introduce new teaching,
but to persuade his readers to stand by the old'.[2] This, it would
seem to me, could equally well be a description of Luke as of the
Pastor. That the Pastor was motivated by pastoral and practical
concerns, that he was not so much an innovative theologian as a
defender of traditional beliefs, is not in dispute. A similar assessment of Luke is, admittedly, debatable. However, although it
clearly enhances the hypothesis of Lucan authorship of the
Pastorals and affords a useful starting point, it is not the mainstay
of the argument. Ultimately, the discussion of specific issues will
be decisive.

In recent years three authors have discussed in some detail the
question of Lucan influence on the Pastorals. C. F. D. Moule[3]
has argued that 'Luke wrote all three Pastoral epistles. But he
wrote them during Paul's lifetime, at Paul's behest and, in part
(but only in part), at Paul's dictation'. Paul dictated the gist of
what he had to say, and Luke freely composed the letters in his
name. In turn this involves the assumption that Paul was released
from his first Roman captivity and did the travelling implied by
the Pastorals before a second Roman imprisonment. In this way
Moule seeks both to explain the similarities and differences

between the Pastorals and other Pauline writings, and to bring them into line with the evidence of Acts. He bases his view on a brief survey of some of the linguistic and thematic connections between Luke–Acts and the Pastorals.

A. Strobel subsequently extended the argument, with a detailed comparison of the language and style of Luke–Acts and the Pastorals.[4] He includes a brief survey of some of the theological affinities, but deliberately emphasizes the linguistic evidence. A serious limitation of Strobel's article, however, is his failure to clarify what he means by Luke as the 'writer' of the Pastorals. He does not tell us whether Luke was an amanuensis, along the lines Moule proposes, or whether he was an independent author. Likewise, he fails to indicate clearly whether Luke wrote them during Paul's lifetime or after his death; nor does he tell us whether they were written before or after Luke–Acts. In an obscure discussion of the relationship between Acts 20.17–35 and 2 Timothy, he seems to suggest that 2 Timothy was written before Acts 20.17–35 and that Luke had first-hand knowledge of Paul's farewell message.[5] This would suggest a thesis similar to Moule's, but it is not certain that this is his intention. This and other weaknesses in Strobel's argument are discussed by N. Brox,[6] who argues emphatically that there is no evidence either for Lucan authorship of, or influence on, the Pastorals. He thinks that Strobel's philological arguments are not compelling, and takes him to task for ignoring the theological and historical problem implicit in his hypothesis. Where there are similarities between Luke–Acts and the Pastorals, he argues, it is because they are rooted in related Pauline traditions of the post-Pauline era.

The argument for Lucan authorship will be presented on three levels. First, the linguistic and stylistic arguments of Moule and Strobel will be summarized, to which little can be added but an assessment of their worth. Second, consideration must be given to the theological and historical arguments for the thesis, since the most that has been done in this respect is the brief comparisons offered by Moule and Strobel, which do not cover many of the crucial issues and rarely discuss in detail those they do cover. Third, it will be necessary to consider objections to the thesis, some of which are raised by Brox, to see if there are reasonable ways of countering them.

What follows, therefore, is an attempt to illustrate and articulate more fully the hypothesis of Lucan authorship and to consider some of the theological and historical problems implicit in it. And, incidentally, if some readers are at the outset not persuaded of the value of such a pursuit, it might be noted that, quite apart from my specific hypothesis, an exploration of the relationship between some of the most important post-Pauline documents in the New Testament is in itself a worthwhile undertaking. Implicitly, of course, I shall be arguing against Pauline authorship at every turn. Indeed, on occasions explicit comparison between Luke, the Pastor, and Paul will simultaneously illustrate the weakness of the Pauline, and the strength of the Lucan, case for authorship.

Before moving to specific themes, it will perhaps be helpful to sketch the particular version of the hypothesis that will be proposed and the presuppositions involved in it. As the argument progresses they will be referred to and explained in more detail. Other hypotheses will be considered in the final chapter.

1 Luke wrote the Pastorals a few years after the completion of Acts.

2 Luke, the author of Luke–Acts, was not Paul's companion of the same name, though he may have had access to material emanating from him. This would explain how he could misplace a genuine Pauline fragment (2 Tim. 4.9–22) in which Paul's companion Luke is mentioned. It would also counter Brox's objections[7] to the use of 2 Tim. 4.11 ('Luke alone is with me') as an indication of authorship, even though they are not overwhelming. For while it may be true that there is no example in ancient pseudepigraphy of a pseudonymous author disclosing his true identity, this does not preclude the possibility that Luke does it here.

3 When he wrote Acts Luke did not have access to Paul's epistles, though he may have known of their existence. Before he wrote the Pastorals, however, he had probably read some of Paul's epistles, most likely 1 and 2 Corinthians and Romans. P. N. Harrison argues that of all the Pauline epistles these are the most frequently echoed in the Pastorals, though he also thinks the Pastor knew Philippians, Galatians, Colossians, Philemon, 1 and 2 Thessalonians and Ephesians.[8] And there is other evidence to suggest that 1 Corinthians and Romans (and Ephesians) enjoyed

wide circulation at an early date.[9] It is also possible to argue that between the writings of Acts and the Pastorals Luke became more familiar with Paul's teaching, but not necessarily in its written form. Either version would explain why, although neither Acts nor the Pastorals are fully in accord with the genuine Pauline writings, the Pauline flavour of the Pastorals is greater than that of Acts. An additional explanation, of course, would be that while in the Pastorals Luke uses the same literary genre as Paul, in Acts he does not.

4   After he had written Acts, Luke gained possession of several travel notes, written by Paul at various points in his career—the so-called 'genuine fragments' of the Pastorals[10]—and used them as the peg on which to hang his pseudonymous letters. As the author of Acts he had already shown considerable interest in the career of Paul, and would naturally search for or be the recipient of further information about him.

5   When he wrote Acts one of Luke's major purposes was to defend Paul and the Pauline communities against Jewish and Jewish-Christian attacks. At that time gnosticism was an incipient danger but not yet a serious threat to the communities for whom Luke wrote, so he mentioned it only in passing (Acts 20.29–30) and as part of Paul's prediction about the future. Between that time and the writing of the Pastorals, however, the influence of the gnostics had increased and they had become the major threat to the Lucan communities. Their influence was particularly insidious, since they claimed Paul as the source of their own teaching. Luke wrote the Pastorals to refute the gnostic misinterpretation of Paul and to show the churches where the source of true authority and sound teaching lay.

Some of these assumptions are debatable, but none of them are inherently improbable. They are, as far as I can see, necessary if one is to argue convincingly for Lucan authorship of the Pastorals. Whether they are adequate remains to be seen.

2

Language and Style

By way of introduction to the following chapters, the linguistic and stylistic evidence compiled by Strobel and Moule can conveniently be assessed at this point.[1] Strobel lists some thirty seven words common to Luke-Acts and the Pastorals but absent elsewhere in the New Testament. In view of the brevity of the Pastorals this is a remarkable total. Consider, for example, that in arguing for the common authorship of Luke and Acts only forty two words shared exclusively by those two works can be adduced. Strobel's total is somewhat exaggerated, for he fails to note that some of these terms are used differently in Luke–Acts and the Pastorals: *anoia* means 'folly' in 2 Tim. 3.9, while in Luke 6.11 it seems to have the rarer meaning 'fury' or 'anger'; *parakolouthein* means 'follow' or 'investigate' in Luke 1.3 and 'appropriate' in 1 Tim. 4.6; 2 Tim. 3.10; *periergos* refers to 'magic skills' in Acts 19.19 and 'busybodies' in 1 Tim. 5.13; *prosklinesthai* means 'join up with' in Acts 5.36, but *prosklisis* means 'preference' in 1 Tim. 5.23. Less significant are the shifts of nuance in terms like *euergesia* (Acts 4.9; 1 Tim. 6.2; cf. Acts 10.38; Luke 22.25) *zoogonein* (Luke 17.33; Acts 7.19; 1 Tim. 6.13) and *sumparaginesthai* (Luke 23.48; 2 Tim. 4.16).

The remaining terms are as follows:[2] *agathoergein/agathourgein* (Acts 14.17; 1 Tim. 6.18; *anapsuxis/anapsuchein* (Acts 3.19; 2 Tim. 1.16); *antilambanesthai* (Luke 1.54; Acts 20.35; 1 Tim. 6.2); *apodechesthai/apodektos/apodoche*—compare Acts 2.41 and 1 Tim. 1.15; 4.9 (cf. Luke 8.40; 9.11; Acts 24.3) and contrast 1 Tim. 2.3; 5.4; *apotheisthai* (Acts 13.46; 1 Tim. 1.19); *acharistos* (Luke 6.35; 2 Tim. 3.2); *buthizein* (Luke 5.7; 1 Tim. 6.9); *dromos* (Acts 13.25; 20.24; 2 Tim. 4.7); *dunastes* (Luke 1.52; Acts 8.27; 1 Tim. 6.15); *exartizein* (Acts 21.5; 2 Tim. 3.17); *epimeleisthai* (Luke 10.34 f; 1 Tim. 3.5; cf. Luke 15.8; Acts 27.3); *epiphainein* (Luke 1.79; Acts 27.20; Tit. 2.11; 3.4); *eusebein* (Acts 17.23; 1 Tim. 5.4);

5

zogrein (Luke 5.10; 2 Tim. 2.26); *kakourgos* (Luke 23.32 f, 39;
1 Tim. 2.9); *meletan* (Acts 4.25—citation; 1 Tim. 4.15); *neoteroi*
(Acts 5.6; 1 Tim. 5.1 f, 11, 14; Tit. 2.6); *nomodidaskalos* (Luke
5.17; Acts 5.34; 1 Tim. 1.7); *nosphizesthai* (Acts 5.2 f; Tit. 2.10);
peitharchein (Acts 5.29, 32; 27.21; Tit. 3.1); *peripoieisthai* (Luke
17.33; Acts 20.38; 1 Tim. 3.13); *presbuterion* (Luke 22.66; Acts
22.5; 1 Tim. 4.14); *prodotes* (Luke 6.16; Acts 7.52; 2 Tim. 3.4);
propetes (Acts 19.36; 2 Tim. 3.4); *puknos* (Luke 5.33; Acts 24.26;
1 Tim. 5.23); *somatikos* (Luke 3.22; 1 Tim. 4.8); *sophrosune* (Acts
26.25; 1 Tim. 2.9; cf. 1 Tim. 3.2; 2 Tim. 1.7; Tit. 2.2–5, 12);
huponoein/huponoia (Acts 13.25; 27.27; 1 Tim. 6.4); *philanthropia*
(Acts 28.2; Tit. 3.4; cf. Acts 27.3); *philarguros* (Luke 16.14;
2 Tim. 3.2; cf. 1 Tim. 6.10).

In addition Strobel lists some twenty-seven terms which occur
in both Luke–Acts and the Pastorals but are rare elsewhere in the
New Testament. Again, it must be observed that not all the
examples are as persuasive as Strobel's simple tally implies. Some
words are used differently: *periistanai* means 'stand around' in
Acts 25.7 and 'avoid' in 2 Tim. 2.16; Tit. 3.9 (cf. John 11.42);
hugiainein is used only in a literal sense in Luke 5.31; 7.10; 15.27
and only in a figurative sense in 1 Tim. 1.10; 2 Tim. 4.3; Tit. 1.9;
2.1 f (cf. 3 John 2); *diamarturesthai* means to 'charge' in 1 Tim.
5.21; 2 Tim. 2.14; 4.1 (cf. Luke 16.28), while its usual meaning in
Acts is to 'testify' (Acts 2.40; 8.25; 10.42; 18.5; 20.21–4; 23.11;
28.23; cf. 1 Thess. 4.6; Heb. 2.6); *analusis* in 2 Tim. 4.6 means
'departure' and while *analuein* in Luke 12.36 may mean the same
(cf. Phil. 1.23),[3] it is usually taken to mean 'return'. Some of the
remaining examples Strobel lists contain only one example of the
word in each set of writings, with one or more examples in the rest
of the New Testament: *adelos/adelotes* (Luke 11.44; 1 Tim. 6.17;
1 Cor. 9.26; 14.8); *anagnosis* (Acts 3.15; 1 Tim. 4.13; 2 Cor. 3.14);
apokeisthai (Luke 19.20; 2 Tim. 4.8; Col. 1.5; Heb. 9.27); *asotos/
asotia* (Luke 15.13; Tit. 1.6; Eph. 5.18; 1 Pet. 4.4); *episkope*
(Acts 1.20; 1 Tim. 3.1; with a different meaning in 1 Pet. 2.12);
presbutes (Luke 1.18; Tit. 2.2; Philem. 9). In cases such as these
one might argue that the single occurrence in each writer with
parallels elsewhere in the New Testament is less weighty than
when there is more than one occurrence in at least one set of
writings. The latter group is as follows: *antilegein* (Luke 2.34;
20.27; Acts 13.45; 28.19, 22; Tit. 1.9; 2.9; cf. John 19.12; Rom.

10.21); *apeithes* (Luke 1.17; Acts 26.19; 2 Tim. 3.2; Tit. 1.16; 3.3; cf. Rom. 1.30); *apistein* (Luke 24.11, 41; Acts 28.24; 2 Tim. 2.13; cf. Rom. 3.3); *aphistanai* (Luke 2.37; 4.13; 8.13; 13.27; Acts 5.37 f; 12.10; 15.38; 19.9; 22.29; 1 Tim. 4.1; 2 Tim. 2.19; cf. 2 Cor. 12.8; Heb. 3.12); *bebelos/bebeloun* (Acts 24.6; 1 Tim. 1.9; 4.7; 2 Tim. 2.16; cf. Matt. 12.5; Heb. 12.16); *brephos* (Luke 1.41, 44; 2.12, 16; 18.15; Acts 7.19; 2 Tim. 3.15; cf. 2 Pet. 2.2); *diaphtheirein/diaphthora* (Luke 12.33; Acts 2.27, 31; 13.34–7; 1 Tim. 6.5; cf. 2 Cor. 4.17; Rev. 4.9); *epiphaneia/epiphanes* (Acts 2.20; 1 Tim. 6.14; 2 Tim. 1.10; 4.1, 8; Tit. 2.13; cf. 2 Thess. 2.8); *ephistanai* (compare especially 2 Tim. 4.6 and Acts 22.30; 28.2; see also 2 Tim. 4.2, the sixteen further uses in Luke–Acts, and 1 Thess. 5.3); *zetesis* (Acts 15.2; 25.20; 1 Tim. 6.4; 2 Tim. 2.23; Tit. 3.9; cf. John 3.25); *metalambanein* (Acts 2.46; 24.25; 27.33 f; 1 Tim. 4.3; 2 Tim. 2.6; cf. Heb. 6.7; 12.10); *nomikos* (Luke 7.30; 10.25; 11.45 f, 52; 14.3; Tit. 3.9, 13; cf. Matt. 22.35); *odunasthai/ odune* (Luke 2.48; 16.24; Acts 20.38; 1 Tim. 6.10; cf. Rom. 9.2); *pagis* (Luke 21.34; 1 Tim. 3.7; 6.9; 2 Tim. 2.26; cf. Rom. 11.9); *perierchesthai* (Acts 19.13; 28.13; 1 Tim. 5.13; cf. Heb. 11.37); *prokoptein* (Luke 2.52; 2 Tim. 2.16; 3.9, 13; Rom. 13.12; Gal. 1.14; cf. *prokope* 1 Tim. 4.15; Phil. 1.12, 25); *spoudaios* (Luke 7.4; 2 Tim. 1.17; Tit. 3.13; cf. Phil. 2.28).

As well as common vocabulary Strobel lists a host of stylistic parallels, not all of which are equally compelling. Some stylistic traits are found almost exclusively in Luke–Acts and the Pastorals and are the kind of quirks which often betray a common hand: *di' hen aitian*, a Latinism (Luke 8.47; Acts 10,21; 22.24; 23.28; 2 Tim. 1.6, 12; Tit. 1.13; cf. Heb. 2.11); *hon tropon de ... houto kai* (Acts 1.11; 27.25; 2 Tim. 3.8; cf. Luke 13.34; Acts 15.11); *epi pleion* (Acts 4.17; 20.9; 24.4; 2 Tim. 2.16; 3.9); *eis to mellon* (Luke 13.9; 1 Tim. 6.19); *dunatos estin* + Acc. + Inf. (Acts 2.24; 2 Tim. 1.12; Rom. 11.23); *hama kai* (Acts 24.26; 1 Tim. 5.13; Col. 4.3; Philem. 22); *ontos* (Luke 23.47; 24.34; 1 Tim. 5.3, 5, 16; 6.19; four times elsewhere in the New Testament). Other traits can be observed which are common to Luke–Acts and the Pastorals but are also found fairly frequently elsewhere in the New Testament. These provide weighty evidence in favour of common authorship but they are not as compelling as those listed above: the impersonal constructs *dei, edei, deon estin* are found thirty three times in Luke–Acts, eight times in the Pastorals, and twenty seven times elsewhere in the New Testament; *dunasthai* is found forty seven times in Luke–Acts, and six times in the Pastorals. Other common constructions are *ou monon de . . . alla kai* (Acts 19.26 f; 26.29; 27.10; 1 Tim. 5.13; 2 Tim. 2.20; 4.8); *lian* (Luke 23.8; 2 Tim. 4.15); *loipon* (Acts 27.20; 2 Tim. 4.8); *ede* (1 Tim. 5.15; 2 Tim. 2.18; 4.6 and twelve times in Luke-Acts); *hosautos* (Luke 13.5; 20.31; 22.30; 1 Tim. 2.9; 3.8, 11; 5.25); *idios* (Luke 6.41, 44; 10.34; 18.28; Acts 1.7; 3.12; 13.36; 28.30; 1 Tim. 2.6; 3.4, 5, 12; 4.2; 5.4, 8; 6.1, 15; 2 Tim. 1.9; 4.3; Tit. 1.3, 12; 2.5, 9); *hikanos* (2 Tim. 2.2; twenty nine times in Luke–Acts; eleven elsewhere); *anagkaios* (Acts 10.24; 13.46; Tit. 3.14; five times elsewhere).

The use of verbs follows roughly the same pattern. Unique parallels are the use of *analambanein* of a person (Acts 20.13 f; 23.31; 2 Tim. 4.11); *pasin . . . phaneron* (Acts 4.16; 1 Tim. 4.15); *mepote* + optative (Luke 3.15; 2 Tim. 2.25); *hina kai autoi* (Luke 16.28; 2 Tim. 2.10); *estosan* (Luke 12.35; 1 Tim. 3.12); and *kekrika* (Acts 16.15; 20.16; Tit. 3.12). Close parallels are to be found too: *apostrephein . . . apo* (Acts 3.26; 2 Tim. 4.4; Rom. 11.26 citation; Heb. 12.25); *arkeisthai* and dative (Luke 3.14; 1 Tim. 6.8; John 6.7; 2 Cor. 12.9); *paristanein* trans. + intrans. (see Acts 1.3 and 2 Tim. 2.15; Acts 27.23 and 2 Tim. 4.17; Rom. 6.13, 16; Eph. 5.27); *prosmenein* + dative (Acts 11.23; 13.43; 1 Tim. 5.5; Matt. 15.32‖Mark 8.2); *ploutein* + *en* or *eis* (Luke 12.21; 1 Tim. 6.18; Rom. 10.12); *pisteuein epi* (Luke 24.25; Acts 2.38; 9.42; 11.17; 16.31; 22.29; 1 Tim. 1.16); *charin echein* (Luke 17.9; Acts 2.47; 7.46; 1 Tim. 1.12; 2 Tim. 1.3; Heb. 12.28; 3 John 4); *boulomai oun* (Acts 17.20; 1 Tim. 2.8; 5.14; cf. John 18.39; Jas. 4.4).

The use of prepositions[4] provides mixed evidence for common authorship. *peri* + acc. and *enopion* occur frequently in Luke–Acts and the Pastorals and not too often in other writers, while *kata* + acc. and *meta* + gen. are common throughout the New Testament. The most striking difference is the absence of *sun* and the rarity of *sun* compounds in the Pastorals, both of which are frequent in Luke–Acts. This is a curious, but not decisive, difference. Not dissimilar is the absence of many particles and conjunctions which are common in Luke–Acts (*ara, achri, ge, dio, eti, heos, idou, hopos, oute, ouchi, plen, te, tote, hoste*). P. N. Harrison[5] thinks this seriously undermines the hypothesis of Lucan authorship. To this Strobel replies that there are some Lucan particles and conjunctions which are found in the Pastorals (*de, gar, kathos, hotan, hote, oun, hos*) and that these parts of speech are mainly tied to the narrative form and the content of Luke–Acts.[6] He notes, for example, that many of the particles and conjunctions absent from the Pastorals are absent from one or more of the Pauline epistles. This is an important point, though it should not be forgotten that, unlike the Pastorals, no single Pauline epistle lacks *all* of these particles and conjunctions!

Finally, we list a few random expressions and ideas shared by Luke–Acts and the Pastorals:[7] *pleroun/plerophorein ten diakonian* (Acts 12.25; 2 Tim. 4.5); *didonai metanoian* (Acts 5.31; 11.18; 2 Tim. 2.25); *theos zon* (Acts 14.15; 1 Tim. 3.15; 4.10); *metalambanein/apodechomai meta eucharistias* (Acts 24.3; 1 Tim. 4.3–4); *krites zonton kai nekron/krinein zontas kai nekrous* (Acts 10.42; 2 Tim. 4.1; cf. 1 Pet. 4.5); *plerousthai charas* (Acts 13.52; 2 Tim. 1.4; cf. Rom. 15.13; the Johannine usage has a distinctive nuance, John 3.29; 15.11; 16.24; 17.13; 1 John 1.4; 2 John 12); *elpida . . . prosdechesthai* (Acts 24.15; Tit. 2.13); *dunasthai arneisthai* (Acts 4.16; 2 Tim. 2.13); *agnoon poiein/kata agnoian prattein* (Acts 3.17; 1 Tim. 1.13; cf. Luke 23.24); *doulos theou* (Acts 16.17; Tit. 1.1; cf. 1 Pet. 2.16; Rev. 7.3; 15.3); *hai hedonai tou biou/hai tou biou pragmateiai* (Luke 8.15; 2 Tim. 2.4). In conclusion, Strobel notes, the Pastorals and Luke–Acts both show a marked preference for compound words of which there are approximately 861 examples in Luke–Acts and 135 in the Pastorals.[8]

We are now in a position to assess the linguistic evidence for common authorship. Strobel notes that the Pastorals have a total vocabulary of 850 words (excluding names) including 175 *hapax legomena*, and that an almost exclusive sharing of approximately 64 terms with Luke–Acts is remarkable. It is pertinent to observe, for example, that of the 540 terms common to Paul and the Pastorals only 50 are typically Pauline, but none of them are shared exclusively with Paul. And in comparison with the 37 terms which the Pastorals share exclusively with Luke–Acts, the next most frequent are 10 shared with Hebrews and 7 with 2 Peter. Weighing these statistics together with the stylistic parallels is no easy task, for there are many factors to be borne in mind. The different length, genre, and subject matter of Luke–Acts and the Pastorals are of considerable significance. Thus Strobel correctly notes that while some 2200 Lucan terms do not occur in the Pastorals, this scarcely belittles the significance of the 64 terms mentioned above for, in view of the brevity and subject matter of the Pastorals, it is more important to observe the similarities than the differences between them. Similarly, the absence of some typically Lucan particles and conjunctions is in large part explicable by reference to the narrative mode and particular subject-matter of Luke–Acts.

A sense of perspective is gained if we remember that even apparently secure hypotheses of common authorship are open to similar objections. Thus while few will be persuaded by A. W. Argyle's arguments against the common authorship of Luke and Acts,[9] it cannot be denied that he has compiled a remarkable list of differences in vocabulary and style between the two documents. And this in turn allows us some leeway in arguing our hypothesis, for it is clear that Luke could show considerable variation in vocabulary and style from one work to another.

It is true, as we noted above, that not all the evidence adduced by Strobel is of equal force. Thus when some terms common to Luke–Acts and the Pastorals are used differently in each set of writings, it argues as much against as for common authorship. And if one counters with the observation that the same term can be used by an author in different ways—compare, for example, *dunastes* in Luke 1.52; Acts 8.27, or *metalambanein* in Acts 2.46; 27.33 f and Acts 24.25—the force of the argument is diminished, but not wholly eliminated. A further complication is that both writers use traditional material. In his Gospel Luke is largely dependent on sources and, though there is little agreement on its precise form and content, that he used traditional material in the composition of Acts is widely accepted. The author of the Pastorals is also dependent on the formulations of his predecessors—summaries of Christian belief, legends about Paul, lists of virtues and vices—not to mention the probability that he incorporates genuine Pauline fragments into his letters and imitates Pauline style as he knew it from some of Paul's writings. And it should be recognized that to assert that Luke and the Pastor depend on sources and tradition has a double-edged effect, since it might be used to reduce the significance of the similarities as well as the differences!

All in all, however, the similarities of vocabulary and style are impressive. It is true that the evidence offered by Strobel cannot be accepted without qualification, but even in somewhat reduced form it shows a remarkable congruence between Luke–Acts and the Pastorals. Maybe it does not in itself compel one to the conclusion that Luke wrote the Pastorals, but it certainly provides strong support for this hypothesis and encourages an attempt to enquire into the theological and historical issues.

3

Eschatology

Eschatology has long been considered a major concern of Luke. I have argued elsewhere that Luke's eschatology is pastorally motivated, and that while in the Gospel there is a tension between a delayed and an imminent parousia, in Acts the imminent strand disappears. There are many who would dispute the existence of expectation of an imminent end in the Gospel, but few who would deny its absence from Acts. There are no positive affirmations of it and at least one warning against it (Acts 1.6–8), though clearly the end will come at some point (Acts 3.23; 17.31).[1] We can confidently assume, therefore, that by the time Luke wrote Acts he no longer expected the end to come in the near future.

Two recent attempts to argue the contrary view are not persuasive. R. Hiers thinks that Luke holds out to his readers the possibility of an imminent end, both by direct statement in the Gospel and by implication in the narrative of Acts.[2] Since for Luke, as for Mark (cf. Mark 13.10), the Gentile mission is a precondition of the end, the natural conclusion is that the end is near. E. Franklin ascribes this view to Luke with even more certainty. The theme is evident, if muted, in the Gospel and must, therefore, be presupposed for the second volume. The theme of universal witness in Acts, which reaches a climax in Rome, means that the 'fact of Acts is therefore an indirect but explicit guarantee of the coming of the end and, in the light of the gospel usage, this is how Luke most likely intended it to be understood'.[3] That some material in the Gospel indicates Luke's belief in an imminent end is, in my view, indisputable. It is doubtful, however, if it is a dominant theme even there and there is certainly no reason to tout it as the key to Acts. For on the one hand there is the remarkable silence of Acts on the question of imminent expectation, and on the other hand the view that Luke 24.47 f and Acts 1.6–8 are designed in part precisely to free the Gentile mission from the

apocalyptic framework found in Mark and, in all probability, in
the teaching of Jesus.[4] Nor can we assume automatically that what
is true for the Gospel is true for Acts, for even if Luke did intend
them to be read as two volumes of a single work, there may have
been an interval between their composition during which he
changed his view on certain issues.

How then does the eschatology of the Pastorals compare with
that of Luke–Acts? The fundamental pattern of most New Testament documents—a tension between realized and futurist eschatology—is to be found in both. R. Bultmann, writing about the
Pastorals, says: 'The paradox of Christian existence—a new existence within this old world (Tit. 2.12)—is here grasped: in other
words the qualitative (and not merely chronological) sense of the
Christian's "betweenness" is grasped'.[5] More important for our
purpose, however, are two further questions: is the futurist
eschatology indefinite or does it include belief in an imminent end;
and, whatever the precise form of this expectation, is it a central or
peripheral theme? The answer to these questions is crucial for a
comparison with the Lucan writings.

There is considerable disagreement on the first question. There
are some who insist that expectation of an imminent parousia is
alive and well in the Pastorals. E. F. Scott, for example, asserts
that the author 'believes that the end of all things cannot be long
delayed', though he remarks cautiously that 'this side of his
thought is not made emphatic'.[6] On the other hand, some scholars
detect a distinct shift away from expectation of an imminent end
in the Pastorals. R. Bultmann's comment is typical: 'Nevertheless,
the present no longer stands in the eschatological tension that Paul
knew; instead the Church has settled down to the prospect that the
world will last a long while yet. When it is time to do so, God will
bring to pass the appearing of Christ ("at the proper time" 1 Tim.
6.15). It is never said that this event lies near ahead, but neither can
one detect such a thing as disappointment at the delay of the
Parousia'.[7]

1 Tim. 4.1 f is the first of two crucial passages which bear on this
issue:

Now the Spirit expressly says that in later times (*en husterois
kairois*) some will depart from the faith by giving heed to
deceitful spirits and doctrines of demons.

It is unclear what exactly is meant by the 'express' words of the Spirit. The subsequent reference to false teachers (vv. 2 f) suggests that the reference is to Christian prophecy since the appearance of false teachers is characteristic of Christian rather than Jewish apocalyptic (Mark 13.22; 2 Thess. 2.3, 11 f; Rev. 13). The phrase *en husterois kairois* is also obscure. W. Bauer suggests that *husterois* is a superlative and translates it as 'in the last times' (i.e., as synonymous with 2 Tim. 3.1), while others who do not translate it thus, nevertheless suggest that this is the meaning.[8] However, apart from the verse in question, Bauer offers no evidence for the superlative meaning and is probably incorrect. The translation 'later times' or 'future times' is preferable.[9]

If we use the translation 'in later/future times' there is not necessarily an eschatological reference. It may simply be a prophecy about the future life of the Church, referring to the time after Paul's departure,[10] and in this case the closest parallel would be Acts 20.29. If it is improbable on linguistic grounds that *en husterois kairois* means 'in the last times', the only justification for interpreting it in this way would be that the content of the prophecy demanded it, i.e., that it was unambiguously apocalyptic. But while false teachers are a sign of the approaching end in some texts (Mark 13.22 etc.), their presence is not always understood in this manner. For example, the activity of false teachers alluded to in Colossians and the Johannine epistles is not taken to be an indication of the nearness of the end. We can conclude, therefore, that the Pastor did not necessarily interpret this prophecy in an apocalyptic manner. It is more likely that he saw it as a prophecy about the future, ongoing life of the Church.

Let us assume for the sake of argument, however, that the apocalyptic interpretation is correct. Does it also imply expectation of an imminent end? Dibelius-Conzelmann comment: 'It is true that formally vv. 1–5 do not make the assertion that the error which was prophesied has now begun (in this respect it is different from 2 Tim. 3.1–6). . . . But the very fact that the mention of the false teaching is directly continued by its refutation (vv. 3–5) shows that the author regards it as a present danger'.[11] If this is so then we must conclude that the author believed that the last days were already present and, according to the standard teaching of Jewish and Christian apocalyptic, that the end was near.

It seems clear that this is the meaning of the second main

passage which bears on this issue, 2 Tim. 3.1–6:

> But understand this, that in the last days there will come times
> of stress. For men will be lovers of self, lovers of money, proud,
> arrogant, abusive, disobedient to their parents, ungrateful,
> unholy, inhuman, implacable, slanderers, profligates, fierce,
> haters of good, treacherous, reckless, swollen with conceit,
> lovers of pleasure rather than lovers of God, holding the form
> of religion but denying the power of it. Avoid such people. For
> among them are those who make their way into households and
> capture weak women, burdened with sins and swayed by
> various impulses.

Here the author begins in the future tense with a prophecy about
the sinners of the last days, illustrating this point with a long
catalogue of vices (vv. 1–5). In vv. 6 f he shifts into the present
tense as he describes his opponents, apparently equating them with
the sinners listed in vv. 1–5. That this implies that the Pastor
believed himself to be living in the last days is generally agreed and,
as in 1 Tim. 4.1 f, this would most naturally be taken as evidence
for the author's belief in an imminent end.

Thus we have one definite and one possible piece of evidence for
the Pastor's belief in an imminent end. How are we to explain it?
Is it an adequate representation of the author's view, or is it simply
a hangover from the past, a careless use of traditional language
that does not express his true beliefs? The latter alternative is
feasible, but it is a type of argument best avoided, since we have no
means of knowing how deliberate the author was in his choice of
language. The problem with the former alternative—that it is an
adequate expression of the Pastor's view—is that it puts considerable weight on one or two passages which do not accord with the
overall tenor of the epistles. For the main emphasis of the Pastorals
is practical, concentrating on the organization and smooth func-
tioning of the Church and the establishment of good relationships
with the world. There is a sense of permanence in the Church's
situation, as if the author saw it having a long future in, and a
stable relationship with, the world. And where there is a theological
emphasis, it is almost wholly on the realization of salvation as
past and present. Dibelius-Conzelmann summarize this neatly:

> The Church has obviously adjusted to the thought of the
> world's duration and has learned to become at home with it.

The presupposition is that salvation has become a reality in the past; salvation in the future appears to be nothing but the shadow of this past epiphany. This consciousness of salvation forms the ultimate essential presupposition of the attitude toward the world which is expressed in the concept of good citizenship.[12]

There is a way out of this dilemma, however, and that is to assume that the Pastor used the phrase 'in the last days' (2 Tim. 3.1 cf. 1 Tim. 4.1) in the Lucan manner. For in Acts 2.17 the same phrase is used in a context where it clearly refers to an extended period of time during which the Spirit is active in the Church and does not imply expectation of an imminent end. As we have seen, futurist eschatology is rare in Acts and hope for an imminent end absent. The 'last days' are thus the era of the Church. There is a variant reading at this point in Acts and E. Haenchen[13] prefers the *meta tauta* of B and LXX to the phrase *en tais eschatais hemerais* in the Western text. However, the Western text is almost certainly correct at this point: in the context of Acts it is the more difficult reading, and scribes were more likely to harmonize with than differ from the LXX. Thus if 2 Tim. 3.1 and 1 Tim 4.1 are interpreted loosely, on the assumption that they use the phrase 'in the last days' in a similar way to Luke, the apparent tension between these verses and the rest of the Pastorals disappears.

At this stage we should consider briefly two other passages which some have taken as evidence for belief in an imminent end:

> I charge you to keep the commandment unstained and free from reproach until the appearing of our Lord Jesus Christ; and this will be made manifest at the proper time by the blessed and only Sovereign, the King of kings and Lord of lords . . . (1 Tim. 6.14–15).

J. N. D. Kelly,[14] who defends Pauline authorship, suggests that these verses show that, 'although Paul fixes no date for this (the parousia) . . . he seems to hint that it may happen in Timothy's lifetime'. This may be so, though one would have to emphasize that it is no more than a hint. That a firm conviction that the end will come (though not necessarily soon) is offered as a comfort and a warning to Timothy is clear. Moreover, in view of the absence of expectation of an imminent end elsewhere in the epistles, and in view of the emphasis on the divine prerogative in choosing the 'proper time' (*kairois idiois*), it is safer to assume that it is not intended here. Indeed it may be the emphasis on divine prerogative, also a common theme in Luke,[15] implies that there was disappointment over the delay of the parousia. This is probably the case in the similar passage in Acts 1.6–7. This disappointment could take the form either of abandonment of belief in a parousia or fervent reassertion of it, including attempts to calculate the exact day. The confident assertion that God will bring about the parousia in his own good time, and not before, could be an answer to either reaction. It has been claimed that in the Pastorals there is no hint of disappointment at the delay of the parousia,[16] and this may be so, for certainly one should be cautious about reading such problems into 1 Tim. 6.15, as one should be cautious in general about reading all positive statements in the New Testament as the answer to a problem or the denial of a heresy! However, it may be that here the Pastor intends an implicit correction of the view that eschatological events, in particular the final resurrection, have already occurred. This is clearly stated to be one of the beliefs of the author's opponents (2 Tim. 2.18) and it may be that the references to a future parousia are intended to counter it. He, like Paul, insists on an eschatological reservation. The connection between gnostic tendencies and belief that resurrection has already taken place can be detected also in Paul's opponents at Corinth, and it may be that in both cases such beliefs arose in response to disappointed apocalyptic expectations. Be that as it may, whatever the original problem was, if there was a problem at all, we can be confident that the text firmly asserts that the end will come, but not that it will come soon.

Kelly implies that the same hope for an imminent end he finds elsewhere in the Pastorals is also evident in Tit. 2.13:

> awaiting our blessed hope, the appearing of the glory of our great God and Saviour Jesus Christ.

This verse, he comments, 'contains a glowing expression of the eschatological expectation of the primitive Church, which impatiently awaited the second coming at the right hand of God. For the writer this expectation is still vivid and real, and this confirms the early date of the letter'.[17] Taken together with Kelly's interpretation of other texts in the Pastorals, one would naturally assume that he thinks this is also evidence for belief in an imminent end. It is possible that the Pastor is here quoting a primitive hymn or liturgy, and in certain contexts there is no doubt that it could be an expression of hope for an imminent parousia. But in its present context there is no suggestion that it refers to an imminent parousia even if that was its original purpose. It does express firmly the conviction that the parousia is coming, but not that it is coming soon (cf. 2 Tim. 4.1). In other words, it is consistent with the other eschatological material we have considered and could be dated equally well at the end of the first century as in the years immediately following Jesus' death.

We can conclude, therefore, that although in the Pastorals there are unambiguous expressions of belief in the parousia, there is no expectation that it will come soon. It remains to assess the importance of this theme. Is it a primary motif, without which the remainder would be a torso? Or is it peripheral, a relic from the past in which the author uses conventional language but with no desire to arouse a lively expectation of the parousia among his readers? These are probably false alternatives neither of which does justice to the evidence. For on the one hand, it is clear that belief in the parousia and an awareness that he was living in the 'last days', are one component of the author's thought. It can be seen as both a threat and a comfort, and it may well be that statements about future eschatological events are a deliberate contradiction of those who claim that these events have already taken place. On the other hand, eschatology is not a dominant theme in the Pastorals. Belief in the parousia gives a certain perspective to the other themes, but it is not the author's central interest. He is far more concerned with the ongoing life of the Church and its members, with their morals, organization, and response to heretical teaching.

It is precisely the same attitude towards eschatology that we find in Acts, for there also it is a visible but inconspicuous theme. And there are many other parallels too. Both Luke and the Pastor believe that there is to be a future parousia, judgement, and resurrection, but not necessarily soon. That this is the view Luke held when he wrote Acts is clear, though he may have held a different view when he wrote the Gospel. Both Luke and the Pastor believed themselves to be living in the 'last days', which they recognized to be a lengthy period of time—though it is highly improbable that either of them expected it to be as long as it has in fact been![18] Thus the overall perspective on eschatology is the same in both writers. Further, we have noted that the most satisfactory understanding of 2 Tim. 3.1 and possibly 1 Tim. 4.1, is a 'Lucan' one. Of course the use of Luke as an analogy should not be overworked, since 2 Pet. 3 (cf. Jude 17; *Did.* 16.3; Barn. 4.9; 12.9; 16.5) uses the phrase 'the last days' (v. 3) with similar imprecision. For while the end will assuredly come (vv. 10 f) it has been delayed with good reason (vv. 4–9).

There are some other linguistic connections which are also worth nothing. Apart from 1 Pet. 4.5, only Luke and the Pastor use the cliché 'the living and the dead' to describe those whom Christ will judge (Acts 10.42; 2 Tim. 4.1; cf. Barn. 7.2; Polyc. *Phil.* 2.1; 2 Clem. 1.1). The Pastorals characteristically use the terms *epiphainein*, *epiphaneia*, *epiphanes* to describe both the parousia (1 Tim. 6.14; 2 Tim. 4.1; Tit. 2.13) and the incarnation (3 Tim. 1.10; 4.8; Tit. 2.11; 3.4), while all other uses of these words in the New Testament, apart from 2 Thess. 2.8, are found in Luke–Acts (Luke 1.79; Acts 2.20; 27.20). One of these refers to the salvation brought by Jesus (Luke 1.79) and another to the day of judgement (Acts 2.20) —though in the former case a hymn, and in the latter case the Old Testament, is being quoted. The comment of Dibelius-Conzelmann illustrates the correspondence: 'The use of the same term "appearance" (*epiphaneia*) for both the past and future appearances of the Lord gives an intimation of the schema of the two advents which is just being developed (similarly in the Lucan writings), although it is not yet conceptually elaborated to its full extent. Here, as in Luke, one finds the characteristic emphasis upon God's authority to establish the appointed time (cf. 1 Tim. 2.6 and Tit. 1.3).'[19]

How then are we to conclude? With respect to eschatology the similarities between Luke–Acts and the Pastorals are such as to encourage the notion of common authorship. To put it more strongly would be to ignore the observation that at the end of the first century their viewpoint was not unique. But the least that must be said is that there is nothing that is inconsistent with the hypothesis of common authorship.

4
Salvation

In considering the theme of salvation in Luke–Acts and the
Pastorals, the natural starting point is a review of their use of *sozo*,
soteria, *soterios*.[1] They are characteristic of both writers, occurring
twenty three times in the Gospel (of which twelve are peculiar to
Luke), twenty times in Acts and ten times in the Pastorals. Many
of the occurrences in Luke–Acts are not directly relevant to our
discussion. Six refer to saving life in a physical sense: Jesus on the
cross (Luke 23.35, 37, 39), and Paul in a shipwreck (Acts 27.20, 31,
34)—with which one can compare the related verb *diasozo* (Acts
27.43–4; 28.1, 4). Eight uses refer to healing (Luke 6.9; 8.36, 42,
48, 50; 17.19; Acts 4.9; 14.9). The ease with which the physical
sense can shift into a more religious sense is evident from Luke
7.50, where the regular healing formula—'Your faith has saved
you'—is used of the woman sinner who has not been healed of any
physical disease. A similar shift is seen in Luke 23.35—'He saved
others, let him save himself'. There are other passages which can
be mentioned briefly: in Acts 7.25 reference is made to the time
when God saved his people through the actions of Moses; and
Luke 1.69, 71 recall Old Testament usage, where salvation is
described in terms of deliverance from one's enemies. None of
these uses is found in the Pastorals which, in view of the subject
matter, is what we would expect.

When we turn to the more specifically theological use of the
terms there are several interesting parallels. Both Luke and the
Pastor speak of salvation as a future event. Luke 13.23 ('Lord will
those who are saved be few?'), associates salvation and entrance
into the future Kingdom (cf. Luke 18.26; Mark 10.26; 13.13, 20).
Luke 9.24 ('For whoever would save his life will lose it; and whoever loses his life for my sake, he will save it') probably refers to
the future (Luke 17.33), and Acts 15.11 reports Peter as saying,
'But we believe that we shall be saved (*sothenai*) through the grace

of the Lord Jesus' (cf. 15.1). 2 Tim. 4.18 associates salvation with future entrance into the Kingdom: 'The Lord will rescue me from every evil and save me for his heavenly kingdom', while 1 Tim. 2.15, which claims that women 'will be saved through bearing children', is probably also a reference to future, eschatological salvation. Finally, we can note a similar allusion in 2 Tim. 2.10: 'I endure everything for the sake of the elect, that they also may obtain the salvation which in Jesus Christ goes with eternal glory'.

At the same time both writers conceive of salvation as a present reality. No clearer assertion could be found than the words to Zacchaeus: 'Today salvation has come to this house, since he also is a son of Abraham. For the Son of man came to seek and to save the lost' (Luke 19.9–10; cf. Luke 9.56, *v.l.*; Luke 4.21 has the same idea without salvation terminology). Similarly, Acts 2.47 says that 'the Lord added to their number day by day those who were being saved (*tous sozomenous*)'. The Pastorals refer to salvation as something which has already been achieved by God on man's behalf and which presumably they now enjoy in the present: 'God, who saved us (*tou sosantos hemas*) and called us with a holy calling' (2 Tim. 1.9); 'he saved us (*esosen hemas*), not because of deeds done by us in righteousness . . .' (Tit. 3.5).

In both cases there are several references to salvation where the temporal reference is either ambiguous or lacking altogether. Thus in 1 Tim. 4.16, 2 Tim. 3.15 the Pastor may intend an eschatological reference but this is not certain. Acts 2.21 ('And it shall be that whoever calls on the name of the Lord shall be saved'), as part of an eschatological prophecy from Joel, might be taken as a future reference, but since Luke clearly sees some elements of this prophecy fulfilled in the present (the Spirit), salvation might be thought of as present too. Many of the occurrences are temporally neutral and describe in a general way the Christian message and its effects (Luke 8.12; Acts 2.40; 4.12; 11.14; 13.26, 47; 16.17, 30–1; 1 Tim. 1.15; 2.4; 2 Tim. 1.9; Tit. 2.11 and probably 1 Tim. 4.16, 2 Tim. 3.15). It is this neutral, non-eschatological sense which is most frequent in both writers and which provides the clearest contrast with Paul, since for him salvation is mainly a future, eschatological term (Rom. 5.9 f; 13.11; 1 Cor. 3.15; 5.5; Phil. 1.28, etc.) even though occasionally he can use it in a present sense (e.g., 1 Cor. 15.2; 2 Cor. 6.12; Rom. 8.24).[2] Thus, as we shall often have cause to observe, Luke–Acts and the Pastorals not only agree with each other, but also differ from Paul.

There are some additional agreements which are worth observing. Both Luke and the Pastor firmly assert that salvation is universal in scope:

'For mine eyes have seen thy salvation
which thou hast prepared in the presence of all peoples,
a light for revelation to the Gentiles,
and for glory to thy people Israel' (Luke 2.30).

'And all flesh shall see the salvation of God' (Luke 3.6).

'I have set you to be a light for the Gentiles, that you may bring salvation to the uttermost parts of the earth' (Acts 13.47).

'. . . this salvation of God has been sent to the Gentiles; they will listen' (Acts 28.28).

God . . . desires all men to be saved and to come to the knowledge of the truth (1 Tim. 2.4).

For the grace of God has appeared for the salvation of all men (Tit. 2.11).

It is true that these universalistic assertions are, in part, differently motivated: in Luke–Acts the context is the Jew–Gentile problem, whereas in the Pastorals it was probably the exclusivism of the gnostic heretics. But this is not their sole motivation and the assertions stand independently of their function as correctives. And the end result is the same, namely that salvation is declared to be open to all men.

On two occasions Luke associates salvation with 'remission of sins', and there is no parallel to this in the Pastorals. However, the connection between the two concepts is not strong, and although both 'remission of sins' and salvation are recurring themes in Acts, they are connected only once.[3] Moreover, according to Acts, 'remission of sins' is a promise made in the context of Christian preaching to non-believers, and since the Pastorals are addressed to Christian believers it is not surprising that the theme is absent here.

The statement that 'there is salvation in no one else, for there is no other name under heaven given among men by which we must be saved' (Acts 4.12) is one with which the Pastor would heartily concur (cf. 1 Tim. 2.5). Yet it is noticeable that neither Luke nor the Pastor shows any great interest in the precise method by which this salvation was achieved. It has frequently been observed that the Lucan writings show little interest in a *theologia crucis*,[4] apart from Luke 22.19b–20 and Acts 20.18. The former is a piece of liturgical tradition, lacking in some manuscripts but probably original, while the latter, which is almost certainly a reference to the atoning work of Christ,[5] is probably a snippet of ecclesiastical tradition too. In both cases, therefore, Luke is repeating traditional material. Presumably he did not find them objectionable for he could easily have omitted them; on the other hand, nowhere does he go out of his way to emphasize their message. Particularly striking is the absence of any reference to the atonement in the sermons in Acts. And even if one makes the most of the association of Jesus with the Servant (Luke 22.37; Acts 8.32; and *pais* in Acts 3.13, 26; 4.27, 30) and the references to him 'hanging on a tree' (Acts 5.30; 10.39; 13.29), as I. H. Marshall does, the most one can conclude is 'that Luke has taken over certain traditions regarding the meaning of the death of Jesus but he has not in any way developed them or drawn attention to them.'[6]

J. N. D. Kelly, writing with the conviction that Paul is the author of the Pastorals, comments: 'The cross, for example, no longer holds the central position he normally accords it'.[7] Indeed, there are only two references in the Pastorals to the atoning significance of Jesus' death:

> For there is one God, and there is one mediator between God and men, the man Christ Jesus, who gave himself as a ransom for all, the testimony to which was borne at the proper time (1 Tim. 2.5–6).

> . . . Jesus Christ, who gave himself for us, to redeem us from all iniquity and to purify for himself a people of his own who are zealous for good deeds (Tit. 2.14).

The first passage echoes Mark 10.45 and is thought by many to be a traditional formula, liturgical in origin, reproduced by the author. In addition it is probable that the emphasis is more on the universality of redemption (cf. 1 Tim. 2.1) than on the method by which it is effected.[8] The second passage also echoes Mark 10.45

as well as some Old Testament passages (Exod. 19.5; Ps. 130.8; Ezek. 37.23). There is no evidence that it is a quotation, but the specific allusion to redemption may simply pick up the phraseology of traditional material such as Mark 10.45; 1 Tim. 2.6. On the strength of these two passages there is some justification for the view that while the author of the Pastorals presents the Christian message in a moralized form, 'the indicative of the Gospel is the basis of the imperative of command'.[9] However it is also true that, unlike Paul, the Pastor does not emphasize or show any special interest in a *theologia crucis* (cf. Gal. 1.4; 2.20; Rom. 3.23 f; 8.32 f; 2 Cor. 5.14; 1 Cor. 15.3). In fact his approach is the same as Luke's: neither of them has an aversion to a *theologia crucis*, since they both allude to it; but when they do, and it is rarely, they merely repeat traditional formulae without any analysis or innovation. By way of contrast it is worth noting that the Lucan tendency to favour a resurrection–exaltation christology over a *theologia crucis* (cf. Acts 5.30–2; 13.22–8) is also found in the Pastorals—a theme to which we shall return when we discuss christology at greater length.

Consonant with their attitude to a *theologia crucis* is the use which Luke and the Pastor make of the central Pauline concepts of righteousness, grace, and faith. Righteousness (*dikaiosune*) and its cognates are used ten times in the Pastorals. In 1 Tim. 3.16 there is a singular usage which accords neither with the normal usage of Paul nor with the other uses in the Pastorals:

> He was manifested in the flesh,
> vindicated in the Spirit,
> seen by angels,
> preached among the nations,
> believed on in the world,
> taken up in glory.

The reference to 'vindication in the Spirit' probably refers to Jesus' resurrection and possibly also to his exaltation, and the unique use of *dikaioo* is doubtless because the author is quoting at this point. 2 Tim. 4.8 also contains a unique reference—to the 'crown of righteousness' which Paul expects as his reward. The phrase has no parallel in Paul whether it is understood as a reward for righteousness or a reward consisting of righteousness.

More significant are the five uses of the concept of righteousness in which it is seen as a virtue. This is particularly clear in the following:

> But as for you, man of God, shun all this; aim at righteousness, godliness, faith, love, steadfastness, gentleness (1 Tim. 6.11).

> So shun youthful passions and aim at righteousness, faith, love and peace (2 Tim. 2.22).

The same use of the term is almost certainly to be found in 2 Tim. 3.16, and the same sense is conveyed by 2 Tim. 1.9, Tit. 1.8 (*dikaios*) and Tit. 2.12 (*dikaios*). Righteousness is not something given, but something to be striven for; it is one human virtue among others. It need hardly be said that this, the characteristic usage of the Pastorals, is quite unlike that which is characteristic of Paul. Tit. 3.5–7 is the only passage akin to Paul:

> He saved us not because of deeds done by us in righteousness, but in virtue of his own mercy, by the washing of regeneration and renewal in the Holy Spirit, . . . so that we might be justified by his grace and become heirs in hope of eternal life.

These verses unquestionably have a Pauline ring to them and yet, as commentators frequently point out, there are subtle and significant divergences. C. K. Barrett summarizes the two sides as follows: 'The expression has a Pauline sound and conveys accurately enough Pauline doctrine; but righteousness (*dikaiosune*) is not used in exactly the Pauline sense ('works of the law' would have been the Pauline phrase) and faith, the Pauline counterpart of works, is not mentioned. It is not unfair to say that faith, man's confident self-abandonment to God's merciful activity, is implied; it remains significant that it is not specifically mentioned'.[10] Dibelius-Conzelmann concur and go on to suggest that 'one might ask whether the act of justification itself is actually meant, or rather a life which is righteous by virtue of grace.'[11] One explanation of this would be that the Pastor had read some of Paul's epistles and, in an attempt to reproduce his teaching on justification, presents a slightly garbled version; but it is perhaps more probable that, as with the other 'faithful sayings' (1 Tim. 1.15; 4.9; 2 Tim. 2.11; Tit. 3.8 and possibly 1 Tim. 3.1), a traditional formula is being quoted. The same is probably true of 2 Tim. 1.9, which also echoes Paul's teaching, even though it is not one of the 'faithful sayings'. The inspiration for 2 Tim. 1.9; Tit. 3.5–7 is clearly Pauline teaching, but the precise formulation is not identical to Paul's own.

The material in Luke–Acts points to a similar conclusion. The term righteous (*dikaios*) is used seventeen times and in a forensic sense (Luke 12.57; 23.47; Acts 4.19), with reference to the resurrection of the just (Luke 14.14; Acts 24.15), as a christological title (Acts 3.14; 4.19; 22.14), and in sayings which contrast righteous men and sinners (Luke 5.32; 15.7; 18.9). However, it is also used to describe a human, albeit religious, virtue of which Luke clearly approves. Thus it is used of Zechariah and Elizabeth (Luke 1.6), Simeon (Luke 2.25), Joseph of Arimathea (Luke 23.50) and Cornelius (Acts 10.22). The verb *dikaioo* and the noun *dikaiosune* in general follow a similar pattern. In Acts 17.31, *dikaiosune* is God's righteousness, *dikaioo* refers to God and Wisdom in Luke 7.29, 35 respectively, and Luke 10.29; 16.15 speak of men 'justifying themselves'. The two remaining groupings are more significant. First, there are several examples of *dikaiosune* being used of human virtue:

> in every nation any one who fears him and does what is right (*ergazomenos dikaiosunen*) is acceptable to him (Acts 10.35).

> And as he argued about justice (*dikaiosune*) and self-control and future judgement, Felix was alarmed (Acts 24.25).

The same sense is probably to be found in Luke 1.75; Acts 13.10, and recalls the dominant use in the Pastorals. Indeed, the correspondence is even more pronounced, for there are two other passages which, like 2 Tim. 1.9; Tit. 3.5–7, echo Paul's teaching but are not a precise reproduction of it. The first is the conclusion to the parable of the Pharisee and the tax-collector:

> 'I tell you, this man went down to his house justified rather than the other; for everyone who exalts himself will be humbled, but he who humbles himself will be exalted' (Luke 18.14).

It is not clear precisely what is meant by 'justified' (*dedikaiomenos*), but it may be an echo of Pauline teaching. The basis of the tax-collector's justification is his plea, 'God, be merciful to me a sinner' (v. 13), and the idea that justification is a gift of God, the result of his mercy, would receive Paul's approval, especially when it is presented as the opposite of the Pharisee's self-justification based on 'works of the law' (cf. vv. 11–12). The allusion is brief, however, and the absence of any reference to faith, together with the concluding references to humility, should make us wary of explicating the message in distinctively Pauline terms. The second example brings us closer since it is part of a speech attributed to Paul:

> 'Let it be known to you, therefore, brethren, that through this man forgiveness of sins is proclaimed to you, and by him everyone that believes is freed from everything from which you could not be freed by the law of Moses' (Acts 13.38–9).

This appears to be a deliberate attempt to echo Paul's notion of justification by faith, yet nothing is said of the basis for this in the death of Christ, and justification is virtually identified with forgiveness of sins. It is unlikely that Luke is attempting to develop a distinctive view, namely that justification through the Law is completed by justification through faith, for that would be 'to impute to him a venture into problems that were foreign to him'.[12] Rather, Luke reproduces a somewhat garbled version of Paul's teaching which he received from tradition and believed to be accurate. The situation is identical to that in the Pastorals: the distinctively Pauline understanding of justification is absent and the concept of righteousness as a virtue takes its place. Where there are deliberate echoes of Paul, and they are rare, the terminology is imprecise.

The use of grace (*charis*) presents a similar pattern.[13] In the Synoptic Gospels Luke alone uses the term. In both Luke–Acts and the Pastorals it can have the profane meaning of 'thanks' (Luke 17.9; 1 Tim. 1.12; 2 Tim. 1.3), but the sense of finding favour with men (Acts 2.47; 4.33) or doing a favour (Acts 24.27; 25.3, 9) cannot be found in the Pastorals, and the epistolary greeting, which accounts for six of the thirteen uses in the Pastorals (1 Tim. 1.2; 6.21; 2 Tim. 1.2; 4.22; Tit. 1.4; 3.15), is of course absent from Luke–Acts.

Grace in the sense of divine favour is found in both Luke–Acts and the Pastorals. The grace of God or Jesus is the basis of salvation (1 Tim. 1.14; 2 Tim. 1.9; Tit. 2.11; 3.7) and the readers are urged to 'be strong in the grace that is in Christ Jesus' (2 Tim. 2.1). The term is used more frequently and diversely in Luke–Acts.

The sense of divine favour is in the first instance dependent upon Old Testament usage (Luke 1.30; 2.40, 52; Acts 7.10, 46), but otherwise the use is varied: Stephen is 'full of grace' (Acts 6.8) and Barnabas sees the grace of God at work in Antioch (Acts 11.23); Christians are urged to continue in divine favour (Acts 13.42; 14.26; 15.40), and grace can characterize the message of salvation (Acts 14.3; 20.24, 32) in association with the performance of miraculous deeds (Acts 14.3 cf. 6.8). Particularly interesting are the echoes of Paul's concept of grace in Luke–Acts and the Pastorals. In Acts 20.24 reference is made to 'the gospel of the grace of God', and in 15.11 Peter asserts that 'we believe that we shall be saved through the grace of the Lord Jesus, just as they will'. The latter saying is not, of course, ascribed to Paul; however, both passages echo the Pauline concept of grace, even if only in passing. Acts 18.27 should be noted too, but even if we translate it, 'he was a great help to those who had come to believe through grace', it adds little to our assessment of 15.11; 20.24, except a connection between faith and grace.[14] Two passages in the Pastorals are closer to Paul (2 Tim. 1.9; Tit. 3.5–7) and another, while somewhat ambiguous, can be read in a Pauline sense (1 Tim. 1.14). The first two passages adopt the Pauline contrast of grace and works and Tit. 3.5–7 connects grace and justification. However, the reference is to 'our works' or 'deeds done by us in righteousness' rather than Paul's 'works of the law', and there is no mention of faith in either verse. Indeed, the concepts of righteousness and grace present us with an identical situation: in each case the terms are used chiefly in a non-Pauline way and, when characteristically Pauline usage is alluded to, precise Pauline terminology is missing. Moreover, in each case the Pastorals come a little closer to Paul's usage than Luke–Acts. If we are to argue for common authorship this could be explained by the assumption that between writing Acts and the Pastorals Luke either had read some of Paul's epistles or had received better information about Paul's teaching.

Before we consider the terms *pistis*, *pisteuein*, we can look briefly at the related term *pistos*. It is used in both Luke–Acts and the Pastorals to mean 'faithful', 'reliable' (Luke 12.42; 16.10–12; 19.17; 1 Tim. 1.12; 3.11; 2 Tim. 2.2, 13). In both singular and plural forms it can also mean 'believers', 'Christians' (Acts 10.45; 16.1, 15; 1 Tim. 4.3, 10, 12; 5.16; 6.2; Tit. 1.6)—a use not found in Paul, except in the variant (and probably secondary) reading in 1 Cor. 7.14. The Pastorals have another distinctive use where *pistos* means 'sure' or 'trustworthy', with reference to a group of epigrammatic summaries of Christian belief known as the 'faithful sayings' (1 Tim. 1.15; 3.1; 4.9; 2 Tim. 2.11; Tit. 3.8). The regular formula introducing the sayings is *pistos ho logos*, and it has probably influenced the similar use of *pistos* in Tit. 1.9. There is only a remote parallel in Acts 13.34, though it is part of a quotation from Isa. 53.3; and the phrase *kai pases apodoches axios* (1 Tim. 1.15; 4.9) finds an interesting parallel in Acts 2.41, *apodechesthai ton logon*. This discrepancy between Luke–Acts and the Pastorals, however, is not a serious or inexplicable one. The faithful sayings in the Pastorals are almost certainly drawn from current church tradition. Their origins may be diverse but they are preserved as a series of summary statements of Christian belief and practice.[15] If Luke wrote the Pastorals one can assume either that he did not know them when he wrote Acts or, if he knew them, that he considered them to be inappropriate to his main theme—the worldwide expansion of Christianity. Conversely, they are particularly appropriate in the Pastorals, where false teachers and disputes over tradition are at issue.

The terms *pistis* and *pisteuein* are used in a similar way in Luke–Acts and the Pastorals. The verb is used frequently in Luke–Acts in the sense 'to be a Christian' (Luke 8.12–13; Acts 2.44; 4.32; 5.14; 13.12, 48; 14.1; 15.5, 7; 17.12, 34; 18.8, 27; 19.2, 18; 21.20, 25; 22.14), or with an object such as God, Jesus, Lord (Luke 1.20, 45; Acts 9.42; 11.17, 21; 10.43; 14.23; 16.31, 34; 19.4; 27.25), the teaching of John and Jesus (Luke 20.5; 22.67), the Old Testament (Luke 24.25), and the early church kerygma (Acts 4.4; 8.12–13). The Pastorals use the verb of belief in Jesus Christ (1 Tim. 1.16; 3.16; 2 Tim. 1.12; Tit. 3.8) or in the sense of being entrusted (1 Tim. 1.11; Tit. 1.3). One noticeable difference is that whereas Acts, like Paul, commonly uses the construction *pisteuein + eis +* accusative, the Pastorals do not. This may in part be because there are relatively few uses of the verb in the Pastorals (only four apart from those meaning 'entrusted').

Faith is used by both Luke and the Pastor to mean the faith, *fides quae creditur* (Acts 6.7; 13.8; 14.22; 16.5; 24.24; 1 Tim. 1.2, 19; 3.9; 4.1, 6; 5.8; 6.10, 12, 21; 2 Tim. 2.18; Tit. 1.4, 13; 3.15). The only comparable absolute use in Paul is in Col. 2.7—if Colossians is considered to be Pauline. The same sense is probably

intended in Phil. 1.27; Gal. 1.23; 5.10, though in each case faith
is qualified by an additional phrase. The shift from Paul to Luke
and the Pastor is twofold: first, faith as *fides quae creditur* is far
more frequent; and second, the absolute use is increasingly the
norm. In passing we should note that, as a result of their polemical
purpose, the Pastorals closely associate, and in some cases virtually
identify, 'the faith' with orthodoxy or sound teaching (1 Tim. 1.19;
4.1, 6; 6.21; 2 Tim. 3.8; Tit. 1.13).

Faith as *fides qua creditur*, often qualified by a phrase like 'in
Jesus Christ', is found in both Luke–Acts and the Pastorals (Luke
18.8; 22.32; Acts 14.27; 20.21; 26.18; 1 Tim. 1.4; 3.13; 2 Tim.
1.5; 3.15; Tit. 1.1) and is, of course, the common usage in Paul.
The special use of faith in miracle or healing stories (Luke 5.20;
7.9, 50; 8.25, 48; 17.5, 6, 19; 18.42; Acts 3.16; 14.9) is not found
in the Pastorals, which is what one would expect, since it is tied
to a particular subject-matter. To a large degree the same can be
said of the use of *pistis* in the Pastorals to signify a virtue (1 Tim.
1.5, 14, 19; 2.7, 15; 4.12; 6.11; 2 Tim. 2.22; 3.10; Tit. 2.2)
associated with other virtues such as love (1 Tim. 1.5, 14; 2.15;
4.12; 6.11; 2 Tim. 1.14; 2.22; 3.10), truth (1 Tim. 2.7), righteousness (1 Tim. 6.11; 2 Tim. 2.22), steadfastness (1 Tim. 6.11;
2 Tim. 3.10; Tit. 2.2), and qualified as 'sincere' (1 Tim. 1.5; 2 Tim.
1.5). This use can also be found occasionally in Paul (1 Cor. 3.13;
2 Cor. 8.7; 1 Thess. 1.3, etc.). The closest parallels in Luke–Acts
are Acts 6.5; 11.24, but the general lack of this usage is explicable
by reference to the different genre and subject-matter of Luke–Acts.
Another use of *pistis* in the Pastorals, where it means 'fidelity'
(2 Tim. 4.7; Tit. 2.16), is found neither in Paul nor in Luke, unless
this is the meaning of Luke 18.8. The remaining distinctive, non-
Pauline use of *pistis*—to mean 'pledge' or 'oath' in 1 Tim. 5.12 and
'proof' or 'assurance' in Acts 17.31—may have slightly different
nuances, but their basic sense is the same and the translation
'pledge' could legitimately be used in both cases. In addition to
the uses of *pistis* in Luke and the Pastor already mentioned, it is
important to note the Pauline uses which they lack. In concluding his discussion of Pauline usage, R. Bultmann says: 'In
particular, however, he brings out the full sense when he sets *pistis*
in antithesis to *erga nomou* and radically develops its character as
hupakoe.'[16] It is precisely these distinctive, central Pauline concepts
which are absent in both Luke–Acts and the Pastorals, for when

they do concur with Paul it is generally with his less distinctive uses.

By way of contrast it will be worthwhile to consider what we might call the approval of natural religion and piety by Luke and the Pastor. This theme partly overlaps with the next chapter and the reader can refer to that as well. Luke's approval of natural goodness and morality is indicated in his addition to the parable of the sower, 'a good and honest heart' (Luke 8.15), his description of Joseph of Arimathea as 'a good and righteous man' (Luke 23.50) and Barnabas as 'a good man' (Acts 11.24), and in the stress on charitable giving which effects inward cleansing, in Luke 11.41. Jewish piety is described approvingly in the birth narratives: Zechariah and Elizabeth are described as 'righteous before God, walking in all the commandments and ordinances of the Lord blameless' (Luke 1.6), and Simeon as a man who was 'righteous and devout' (Luke 2.25, cf. 2.37). The Ethiopian eunuch, who in Luke's eyes was certainly a Jew,[17] is portrayed as a devout man, travelling to Jerusalem to worship (Acts 8.27). Luke views the Gentiles in the same way. The centurion whose child is sick is represented by local Jewish leaders who explain to Jesus that the centurion is 'worthy to have you do this for him, for he loves our nation, and he built us our synagogue' (Luke 7.4–5). Jesus responds and heals the child. Cornelius is reputed to be 'a devout man who feared God with all his household, gave alms liberally to the people, and prayed constantly to God' (Acts 10.2, 22) and, as a result, becomes the first Gentile to hear the gospel (Acts 10.4). Subsequently, when Peter arrives on the scene, he declares: 'Truly I perceive that God shows no partiality, but in every nation any one who fears him and does what is right is acceptable to him' (Acts 10.34–5). The speech of Paul in Athens (Acts 17.22–31) also contains a magnanimous and positive assessment of Gentile piety and worship. It is true that their idolatry is criticized, but it is constructive criticism, an attempt to point them in the direction of the God whom they are unwittingly worshipping and to the kind of worship appropriate to him.[18] Gentile piety (*eusebeia* 17.22), is laudable, though misguided. God overlooks their ignorance and now calls them to repentance in the face of future judgement (17.30–1).

How are we to assess Luke's view as expressed in these verses? It is true that in the majority of cases where Luke praises upright behaviour and piety these are seen, in part, as a kind of preparation for Christian faith (Luke 1.67–9; 2.28–32, 38; 7.9; Acts 8.36; 11.17; 17.30–1).[19] It is also true that Luke does not have a theory of salvation by works or piety, even though he comes close to it in Acts 10.35; 13.39. However, this is not so much because he can be shown to hold the opposite view of salvation by grace (Acts 15.11; 20.24), but rather because, put in those terms, it was not a problem which concerned him. He shows no sign of tussling with the problem on any profound level. His attitude was simple and pragmatic. Good behaviour and natural piety, whether exhibited by Jews or Gentiles, Christians or non-Christians, were qualities which Luke approved of and which he believed God approved of too.

In the Pastorals the same overall view is to be found. As we shall see there is a sense in which much of their ethical teaching is neither specifically Christian nor motivated by a specifically Christian theology. Indeed, the motivations are often quite explicitly pragmatic. One theme which constantly crops up in the Pastorals is the demand for good works (*ergon* with *agathon* 1 Tim. 2.10; 5.10; 2 Tim. 2.21; 3.17; Tit. 1.16 or with *kalon* 1 Tim. 5.25; 6.18; Tit. 2.7, 14; 3.8, 14). The exhortation is regular and insistent, though tempered somewhat by 2 Tim. 1.9; Tit. 3.5–7, which assert that works are not the basis of salvation. Even so, the imperative is not unambiguously based on an indicative, as is clear from what are sometimes called the 'Pelagian' passages in the Pastorals. In 1 Tim. 1.13–16 Paul's career as a persecutor and enemy of God and the Church is excused on the grounds of ignorance. He receives divine mercy because of his ignorance and because God wants him to be an example. In 1 Tim. 2.15 there is an obscure and ambiguous statement: 'Yet woman will be saved through bearing children, if they continue in faith and love and holiness, with modesty'. It is not clear whether 'woman' refers to women in general or to Eve, whether 'salvation' is eternal or temporal, whether 'bearing children' refers to childbirth in general or the birth of Jesus, or whether 'they' refers to women, a husband and wife, or to children.[20] It is most probable that the author's concern is with the role of women in general and that he is suggesting that to achieve eternal salvation they should concentrate on bearing and raising children (cf. 1 Tim. 5.10; Tit. 2.2–5) as well as continuing in the Christian faith. The latter demand tempers, but does not wholly remove, the suggestion of salvation by 'works', especially since faith, love, holiness, and modesty themselves recall the other lists of virtues in the Pastorals. A similar suggestion is made in 1 Tim. 6.18–19, where the wealthy are exhorted to perform good deeds in order to guarantee 'a good foundation for the future, so that they may take hold of the life which is life indeed'. Finally we note that in 2 Tim. 2.19 f the Pastor urges his readers to moral effort. Using the metaphor of household vessels, he exhorts them to 'purify themselves' for noble use by the master of the house—an exhortation which is then expanded in v. 22: 'So shun youthful passions and aim at righteousness, faith, love, and peace. . . .' It is not impossible to harmonize such statements with 2 Tim. 19.1 and Tit. 3.5–7, but there is no doubting an ambiguity and looseness of expression which is as like the view of Luke as it is unlike the view of Paul.

In the next chapter we shall discuss the use of *eusebeia* and cognates in the Pastorals, and clearly it is relevant here too. It is a term which characterizes the Hellenistic ideal of a devout, pious man and the Pastor uses it in this way, adapting it only in the sense that the object of piety is the Christian deity. The Pastor clearly approves of *eusebeia*, but assumes that the divine approval sought by this piety is that of the Christian God. There is one other interesting passage to be considered. In 2 Tim. 1.5 the Pastor writes:

> I am reminded of your sincere faith, a faith that dwelt first in your grandmother Lois and your mother Eunice and now, I am sure, dwells in you.

In Acts 16.1 it is mentioned that Timothy's mother was a Christian Jewess and his father a Greek, but no mention is made of his grandmother. Some commentators suggest that we are meant to assume that both mother and grandmother were Christians.[21] However, in view of the reference to the piety of Paul's Jewish forebears (v. 3), there is no reason to suppose that the reference is specifically to Timothy's Christian upbringing. It is rather to the fact that he has grown up in a religious family, where the influences were both Jewish and Christian. That is to say, no distinction is made between Christian and Jewish piety. Indeed, one might go on to say that it is not even Jewish and Christian piety which are welcomed, but piety *per se* in whatever context. That Timothy's background is both Jewish and Christian is incidental. The importance of this religious training is emphasized later, when the author alludes to Timothy's knowledge of the Scriptures (1 Tim. 3.15). This is not to say, of course, that the Pastor believed that the pious Jew or pagan had no need of Christian belief, but it is clear that he approves of piety in all its manifestations and considers it to be an invaluable preparation for Christian belief. Finally, while we are on the topic of the religious upbringing of Paul and Timothy (2 Tim. 1.3, 5; 3.15), we can note that these passages say neither more nor less than the equivalent passages in Acts 23.1; 24.14 f; 26.6, 22 f, where Paul refers to his forebears. The continuity of the old and the new eras is implicit in both and one need read neither more nor less of a *heilsgeschichtliche* concept into the passages in 2 Tim. than into those in Acts.[22]

To summarize: we have found that Luke and the Pastor have the same understanding of the concepts of salvation and share a similar attitude towards a *theologia crucis*. Moreover, their use of the concepts righteousness, grace, and faith is remarkable not only for the similarity between them but for their consistent disagreement with Paul. In addition, Luke and the Pastor have the same attitude towards morality and piety. There is a certain tension between their allusions to salvation by grace and salvation by works—a tension which exists, however, precisely because we place them side by side with the distinctive and unambiguous opinions of Paul. Both authors seem vaguely aware of Paul's stance and allude to it in language which comes close to that of Paul himself; but neither of them seems aware of the potential contradiction between this and their demand for, and approval of, good works. It is true that Luke uses the phrase 'good works' only once (Acts 9.36), but there is enough related evidence to indicate that he shares the same view as the Pastor even though the latter's emphasis on this theme may in part be a deliberate contrast with the futile speculation encouraged by the heretics. With respect to piety (*eusebeia*) or 'natural religion', Luke and the Pastor also agree. Piety, whether exhibited in Jews, pagans, or Christians, is seen as a laudable virtue in its own right and can also serve as a valuable preparation for Christian faith.

Such an attitude is, of course, in marked contrast with Paul's view. In Phil. 3.4 f Paul enumerates his reasons for 'confidence in the flesh': family pedigree, fulfilment of the law, training as a Pharisee, and zeal as a persecutor. But, he continues, 'whatever gain I had, I counted as loss for the sake of Christ' (v. 7) in order that he might have 'not a righteousness of my own, based on law, but that which is through faith in Christ, the righteousness from God that depends on faith' (v. 9). Whereas for Luke and the Pastor a Jewish religious training is potentially the first step on the way to salvation, for Paul it is 'counted as loss', part of that other righteousness which is based on the law. With respect to Gentile piety Paul is no less radical. In Romans 1—3 he discusses the issue of Gentile and Jewish religiosity. While he is aware that there are some advantages to being a Jew (Rom. 3.1 f.) and that, in theory at least, some Gentiles might fulfil the intention of the law without knowing the letter of the law (Rom. 2.14 f), his judgement on the situation is in reality comprehensive and bleak: 'all men, both Jews and Greeks, are under the power of sin' (Rom. 3.9); 'all have sinned and fall short of the glory of God' (Rom. 3.23). In other words, both Jewish and Gentile religiosity prepare for Christian belief not in the sense that there is a valuable continuity, but only in the sense that they leave all men condemned in God's eyes and wholly dependent on his mercy. Again, we can conclude that Luke and the Pastor not only agree substantially with each other but also fail to capture the essence of Paul's teaching. I would suggest, moreover, that the similarities are such that not only are they consistent with, but also suggest, the view that Luke wrote the Pastorals.

5

The Christian Citizen

We shall now consider two closely related themes: the attitude towards the State and the overall ethical stance in Luke–Acts and the Pastorals. We shall also compare them with Paul and this will serve not only to accentuate their difference from him but also their similarity to each other.

In Luke–Acts there is no formal statement on the relationship between Church and State, which is to be expected in the narrative genre; but the narratives do have a pedagogical purpose. They instruct by example and thus implicitly contain messages for the reader about the nature of true Christian behaviour. In Luke's Gospel, more emphatically than in Mark and Matthew, Jesus' innocence with respect to Roman Law is proclaimed.[1] Three times during his trial Pilate declares that he is innocent (Luke 23.4, 14, 22) and this conviction is reiterated by the thief on the Cross (Luke 23.41). Whereas the centurion in Mark declares, 'Truly this man was the son of God' (Mark 15.39), in Luke he says, 'Truly this man was innocent' (Luke 23.42), and the charges on which he was arraigned (Luke 23.2) are unambiguously dismissed as false (Luke 20.20 f, 36; 23.14). This emphatic declaration of Jesus' innocence confirms hints earlier in the Gospel of the apolitical character of Jesus' ministry (Luke 4.16 f; 9.7 f; 13.31 f; 19.28 f) and, conversely, implies that it is Jesus' Jewish accusers who are seditious and untrustworthy.

Acts conveys an identical message: Jesus' innocence is confirmed in the apostolic kerygma (Acts 3.13; 13.28); Cornelius, a Roman centurion, becomes a Christian (Acts 10—11), as does the proconsul of Paphos (Acts 13.6–12); the magistrates in Philippi are temporarily bulldozed into maltreating Paul and Silas, but eventually they free them with apologies (Acts 16.19–40); Gallio quickly perceives that the Jewish accusations against Paul are based on issues in Jewish and not Roman law, and he dismisses the charge (Acts 18.12 f). In Acts 22—3 it is the Romans who rescue Paul from a maddened Jewish mob and an attempted ambush, while the tribune, Claudius Lysias, reaches the same conclusion as Gallio—Paul is innocent under Roman law. Under pressure from Paul's Jewish accusers Felix keeps Paul in prison (Acts 24.27) but it is a relaxed form of detention (Acts 24.23). Paul unambiguously declares his innocence before Festus: 'Neither against the law of the Jews, nor against the temple, nor against Caesar have I offended at all' (Acts 25.8), and he insists on a trial before Caesar after Festus has found him innocent but, like Felix, has bowed to Jewish pressure (Acts 25.9, 18–19, 25). Agrippa makes the same declaration of innocence, noting that but for his appeal to Caesar Paul could have been freed. The centurion in charge of Paul on the way to Rome treats him well (Acts 27.3, 43) and when they arrive Paul is detained under a loose form of house-arrest which allows unhindered preaching (Acts 28.16, 30–1).

It is this series of stories which makes up Luke's political apologetic in Acts. Certainly, it is scarcely conceivable that he intended Roman readers to find an implicit political apologetic in his portrayal of Jewish–Christian relations—either that the Church is part of Judaism and therefore should be considered a *religio licita*, or that it is distinct from Judaism and thus has no part in the Jews' subversive activities. Conzelmann writes: '. . . the relationship of the Church to Israel belongs to an entirely different category than that of political apologetic. It is never used in argument with the Romans. It belongs to the dispute of the Church with Israel and only there'.[2] What then is Luke implying? First, it is implicit in the narratives of Acts that Christians need to work out an attitude towards the State. The State is here to stay; it *is* the political reality, and some adjustment to it has to be made. As Luke sees it this is a relatively simple problem. Observing the example of Jesus and Paul it is clear that the Church has nothing to fear from the Romans. They already have good relations with the Romans and certainly there is no cause to quarrel with them. The Romans had never found fault with either the founder or the chief missionary of the Church; indeed they had categorically asserted their political innocence. Their treatment of Paul, for example, was in the main kind and respectful, their one weakness being a tendency to succumb to Jewish pressure without which he would never have run foul of them. On the other hand, but for Roman protection, Paul would have been lynched by Jewish mobs. So far the message is simple and uniform. But there are two caveats. First, it was clear that for all their good intentions, the Romans were ultimately responsible for the deaths of Jesus and Paul. The latter's death is, of course, not mentioned—an eternal puzzle to commentators. However, it can scarcely have been unknown to Luke's readers that Paul had finally been put to death by the Romans; and even though it is not part of the drama, it casts a shadow from offstage. Second, there are the two statements which place a limitation on the Christian's obedience to political authorities:

> But Peter and John answered them, 'Whether it is right in the sight of God to listen to you rather than to God, you must judge; for we cannot but speak of what we have seen and heard' (Acts 4.19–20).

> But Peter and the apostles answered, 'We must obey God rather than men' (Acts 5.29).

It is true that the disciples were forced to this extreme expression of their loyalties by Jewish and not Roman authorities, but they nevertheless voice a clear and unambiguous general principle. When the demands of God and man conflict, there is no doubt which way Christians should decide. Thus while the Romans did not instigate action against Jesus or the Church and proclaimed their innocence under Roman law, under pressure they did assent to the deaths of Jesus and Paul. Likewise, while there was no reason to suppose that under normal circumstances being a Christian would involve running foul of civil authorities, if it did, the prior demand was that of God.

The crucial question we now have to ask is, to whom is Luke addressing himself? It has been suggested frequently that it is Roman readers, and in particular Roman officials, that he has in mind. The point of the statements we have surveyed would then be to inform contemporary officials of the political innocence of Christianity and to urge them to follow the example of their predecessors in treating the Church with consideration and respect. With reference to a more limited view, namely that the purpose of Acts was to provide the Romans with an apology for Paul, C. K.

Barrett comments: 'No Roman official would ever have filtered out
so much of what to him would have been theological and ecclesiastical rubbish in order to reach so tiny a grain of relevant apology'.[3]
While such a severe judgement is less readily applicable to the
more general theme of political apologetic—since a considerable
portion of Acts has a bearing on it—the main objection still stands.
Luke's purpose cannot have been solely to provide political
apologetic for Roman ears; he must at the same time have been
trying to inform them about the history of the Church and convince them of the truth of what might have seemed to be 'theological and ecclesiastical rubbish'. Indeed, such an evangelical
purpose for Acts is touted by J. C. O'Neill.[4]

A far more convincing explanation of the political theme in Acts
is to assume that it is addressed primarily to Christian readers and
not to Roman officials. Indeed, it has recently been suggested, with
particular reference to Pilate, that his indifference to serious charges
and legal procedures would more likely have led later Roman
officials to condemn him for inefficiency than to use him as an
example.[5] And at any rate, an interpretation that sees the primary
audience as Christian readers makes far more sense of the rest of
Luke–Acts. On this view the message would be that the Roman
authorities are just and fair; they treat all citizens with impartiality
and will not allow anyone to be arraigned on false charges. Christians have no need to fear civic authorities, and if they get on quietly
with their own business, Rome will leave them alone. The great
figures of the past stand as examples of good Christian citizenship.
However, if things go awry, and there is an attempt by political
authorities to ban them from confessing and propagating their
faith, they are bound to stand by their prior commitment to God.

Luke's motivation in taking up this stance was varied. One
important factor was the pragmatic observation that the Romans
provided firm and orderly government and thus encouraged a
stable social and political environment in which Christianity
could expand. And, since on the whole the Romans were fair in
their treatment of the Church, confrontation with them would be
both useless and counter-productive. There was probably a more
profound factor motivating Luke as well: the loss of belief in an
imminent parousia. While in the Gospel it is arguable that hope
for an imminent end is still alive, in Acts it is clearly absent. The
consequence of this was a radical change in perspective, for both

Church and State were here to stay: 'Whereas in the original
eschatological perspective it was felt that the State had to be with-
stood, now the attempt is made to enter into conversation with it,
in order to achieve a permanent settlement.'[6]

The message of the Pastorals is almost identical. In the first
instance, it is implied by 2 Timothy that Paul is innocent of any
serious charge. He is a prisoner in Rome, but only because of his
commitment to the Christian gospel (2 Tim. 1.11–12). No other
information is given about the reasons for Paul's imprisonment,
though it is indicated that his first defence has been successful
(2 Tim. 4.16–17) and that his detention does not preclude visits
from friends and the writing of letters (2 Tim. 4.9 f, cf. Acts
28.30–1).

In 1 Tim. 2.1 f and Tit. 3.1 f both obedience to and prayers
for secular authorities are urged upon the readers. 1 Tim. 2.1 f
reads:

> First of all, then, I urge that supplications, prayers, inter-
> cessions, and thanksgivings be made for all men, for kings and
> all who are in high positions, that we may lead a quiet and
> peaceable life, godly, and respectful in every way. This is good,
> and it is acceptable in the sight of God our Saviour, who desires
> all men to be saved and to come to the knowledge of the truth.

There are several parallels to these statements about prayers for
rulers, especially in Jewish literature (Ezra 6.10; 1 Macc. 7.33;
Philo, *In Flacc.*, 49: Jos., *War*, II, 197, 408 f). For Jews such
prayers were a substitute for Emperor worship and were thus their
expression of loyalty to the government. The purpose of such
prayer for Christians, according to 2 Timothy, seems to be twofold: to allow Christians to lead godly and quiet lives, presumably
because they were thereby fulfilling their civic duty and supporting
the stability of Roman rule (v. 2); and to enhance the opportunities
for evangelism, presumably by helping to create a stable social and
political environment in which it could thrive (vv. 3–4).

In a similar statement, Titus is urged to:

> Remind them to be submissive (*hupotassesthai*) to rulers and
> authorities, to be obedient (*peitharchein*), to be ready for any
> honest work, to speak evil of no one, to avoid quarrelling, to be
> gentle, and to show perfect courtesy to all men (Tit. 3.1–2).

This command is different from 1 Tim. 2.1 f, but the motivation and spirit are the same. There may be some relation between the command and the Cretans' notorious turbulence (Tit. 1.5; Polybius, *Hist.* IV, 46), but clearly it also has a broader significance. Christians are urged to be obedient to civic authorities and to lead honest, hard-working, and law-abiding lives. No rationale is offered; it is a simple, direct, and unambiguous command. The use of the two verbs *hupotassesthai* and *peitharchein* reinforces the absolute nature of the command, and apparently no exceptions are envisaged. Some have proposed, however, a more flexible interpretation. C. E. B. Cranfield suggests that *hupotassesthai* here (as in Rom. 13.1) means 'reciprocal respect', 'a recognition that the State has a greater claim on me than I have on myself'—a nuance of the verb he finds, for example, in Eph. 5.21 and Col. 3.18, and transfers to Rom. 13.1 and Tit. 3.1. He argues further that a more rigid interpretation of Tit. 3.1; Rom. 13.1 contradicts the critical stance of other documents (e.g. Acts 5.29; Rev. 13—14).[7] The latter argument is persuasive only if one assumes, as I would not, that the New Testament has a uniform view on the matter. The use of Eph. 5.21 and Col. 3.18 as analogies is also to be questioned, since the contexts are quite different and, as G. Delling says, 'In exhortation the middle embraces a whole series of meanings from subjection to authority on the one side, to considerate submission to others on the other. As regards the detailed meaning this can finally be decided only from the material context'.[8] Others suggest that *hupotassesthai* means to recognize and accept the general relationship of subordination of the State, but not to obey all its commands regardless of their nature. Likewise it is proposed that the use of *peitharchein* implies that the State had not yet demanded Emperor worship from the Church or made any similar demands that would cut at the roots of Christian belief.[9] The latter supposition is probably correct, and it may well be that the Pastor would have approved of disobedience to the State under certain circumstances. But he does not say this, nor does he seem directly to consider the possibility of such circumstances arising. His command, as it stands, is absolute.

Another theme relevant to the Pastor's attitude towards the State is the constant exhortation that believers should be honourable, peaceful, and responsible citizens. He seems convinced that Christians should integrate with society and cause no offence. Thus the ethical demands placed on a Christian are the same as for any good citizen: 'The Christian orientation of this ethic is of course still obvious, since reference is always made back, in some way or other, to Christ or to the Christian tradition; but this orientation is definitive for the character of the ethics only where it provides for an endorsement of certain social institutions. . . .'[10] Another illustration of the Pastor's eagerness for the integration of Christians with society are the commands to do nothing that will jeopardize the reputation of the Church in society (1 Tim. 3.7, 12; 5.10, 14; 6.1; Tit. 1.6 f, 28; 3.1, 8, 14).

So far we have found a consistent attitude towards civic authorities in the Pastorals. But there is one jarring note. For, implicitly at least, there is a limit to the Christian's integration into society and it is sharply illustrated in the fact of Paul.[11] He refers to his constant suffering as a Christian apostle and, according to 2 Tim. 4, is on the verge of martyrdom, thus creating a tension between the ideal expressed for Christians in general and the particular fate of Paul. The message seems to be that under normal circumstances a believer's aim should be to live as a responsible, sober, and upright citizen, to pursue those virtues that were highly prized in society and thus win their respect and acceptance. In socio-political terms, what was required of a Christian was required of all good citizens. However, there was no guarantee that this ideal relationship would be allowed to prevail, and the believer's integration with society should not be allowed to compromise his profession of faith. As the lives of both Jesus (1 Tim. 6.13) and Paul (2 Tim. 1.8 f; 4.6) if ndicated, persecution, even martyrdom, was always a possibility. Christians were not to provoke or encourage enmity, but when it arose they were to follow the example of Jesus and Paul and stand firmly by their beliefs.

What was the Pastor's motivation in proposing such a relationship with the State? In part, the encouragement of a peaceful, respectable existence may have been a rejection of gnostic enthusiasm and some of the excesses it could lead to. Believers are urged to avoid the disputes and wrangling which characterize the heretics and disrupt the peace of the Church.[12] In addition it is clear that, like Luke, the author has a quite pragmatic motive, namely to encourage a stable and peaceful environment in which the Church can both exist and expand (1 Tim. 2.2–4). Furthermore, there is the evident decline of an expectation of an imminent end. The State and the Church are here to stay and must accommodate each other. The Church could no longer view the State as an irrelevance, part of that world order which was rapidly passing away and would disappear with the imminent advent of the Kingdom; it was a political and social reality which could not be ignored and to which it had to adjust.

How do Luke and the Pastor compare in their attitude towards the State? In all essentials they are the same. Both address themselves primarily to Christian believers and commend the establishment of a peaceful, working relationship with the State. Both imply that, as a rule, confession of Christian belief is not incompatible with civic obedience. On the other hand, both are aware of the limits to this obedience as illustrated in the career of Jesus and, more especially, in the career of Paul. They are examples not only of the persecution and suffering that could attend Christian belief, but also of the firm refusal to compromise their faith. It is particularly interesting that in both writers there is an unresolved tension between the ideal of civic obedience and Roman justice and the fate of Paul. In addition, it is evident that both authors recognize that when things do go awry and the State turns against the Church it is not catastrophic; for overruling all is the plan of God, who ensures that the spread of the gospel is unimpeded (Acts 28.30–1; 2 Tim. 4.16–18). It is remarkable too that neither writer offers a theory of Church-State relationships. The appropriate behaviour is not debated, but encouraged by example or straightforward exhortation.

The motivations of Luke and the Pastor are likewise similar. Both writers are keen to maintain the socio-political conditions which best serve the needs of Christian evangelism, and at the same time they share an underlying and more fundamental motivation, namely the need for the Church to adjust its attitude towards civic responsibility in line with its revised eschatological expectations.

So far we have found no important differences between Luke and the Pastor. C. K. Barrett suggests one distinction: 'The Pastoral epistles, which in many respects reflect the same background and motivation as the Lucan writings, make a similar though not identical point. . . . Luke argues that, historically, the State has no reason to suspect, much less to persecute, the Church; the author of the Pastorals urges Christians to give no unnecessary provocation'.[13] As it stands such a distinction would not be incompatible with the theory of common authorship. It would be a difference of emphasis but there would be no difficulty in supposing that the same man wrote both. However, if the object of Luke's attention in Acts is Christian readers rather than Roman officials, the contrast disappears. Both authors encourage their readers not to fear but to respect and serve the State, to be law-abiding and responsible citizens.

A brief comparison between the views of Luke and the Pastor and Paul will serve to accentuate their similarity to each other and difference from Paul. Romans 13.1–7 is the *locus classicus* for Paul's view. It opens with the statement:

> Let every person be subject to the governing authorities. . . .

The verb used is *hupotassesthai* and, although it is not reinforced with *peitharchein* as in Tit. 3.1, it still implies a call for unqualified submission to the Roman State. There is no suggestion of any limit to the obedience owed to civic authorities.[14] There is no reason to suppose that Paul's use of the indicative rather than the imperative to describe the responsibilities of the State implies that it can be disobeyed if it fails to fulfil its object of repressing evil and doing good.[15] Nor does the reference to conscience in v. 5 suggest that Christian obedience should be critical and unpredictable, an obedience which is withheld when Christian service becomes impossible in a particular setting.[16] It may be that the special circumstances of the Roman Church[17] or the excesses of zealots motivated Paul's statement,[18] but his statement remains clear—obedience without qualification. It is true that Paul would not have exhorted Christians to deny their faith because the State demanded this, any more than he would have expected a wife to commit adultery because her husband commanded it (Col. 3.18); but in Rom. 13.1–7 Paul does not appear to envisage such problems and his exhortation is unambiguous. In this respect he agrees with the major emphasis of Luke and the Pastor, but he does not envisage the limitations they imply. Another difference is that Paul offers a theoretical justification for his stance (cf. 1 Pet. 2.16–17): first, all authority, including political authority, comes from God (vv. 1–2); second, as the instruments of God's wrath, rulers need be feared only by the wicked (vv. 3–4); and third, for the sake of conscience (v. 5). Moreover, as Rom. 12.2; 13.11–12 indicate,

Paul had a more dialectic view of eschatology. There is no indication that he had abandoned belief in an imminent end and that
this forced him to come to terms with the State and its demands.
Indeed, if his eschatological views did motivate his stance in
Rom. 13.1–7 it was in a quite different way. One might argue that
it is precisely because he believes the parousia to be imminent that
he recommends submission to the State. Christians can afford
absolute obedience, since the State is part of the world-order which
is rapidly passing away.[19] Alternatively, one might argue, by
analogy with one interpretation of 2 Thess. 2.6 f, that it is
because the State restrains evil and delays the parousia that
Christians should obey it, since this allows more time for preaching
the gospel.[20] However that may be, it is clear that the eschatological motivation and the theoretical underpinning distinguish
Paul from Luke and the Pastor.

We shall now turn to some other aspects of Christian citizenship
as they are expressed in the general ethical teaching of Luke and
the Pastor. Clearly we face a problem here, since the very nature
of the Gospel and Acts makes it difficult to extract a distinctive
Lucan ethic. The Gospel is largely composed of pre-Lucan
material, albeit reshaped by the author, and thus only a limited
amount provides evidence for a distinctive Lucan viewpoint. Acts
probably also uses sources but, more importantly, since it is cast in
narrative form it is unlikely to provide much in the way of specific
ethical teaching or exhortation. The Pastorals, on the other hand,
contain a considerable amount of ethical exhortation which is
appropriate both to the epistolary genre and to the particular
situation being addressed. A comparison between Luke and the
Pastor on this score is thus difficult but not, I think, impossible.

First, we can compare the motivations and principles on which
their ethical stance depends. It is clear that in Paul's writings, for
example, the imperative of command springs from and is moulded
by the indicative, for the indicative expresses what has already
been realized through the death and resurrection of Jesus. Yet
Paul always retains what has been called an 'eschatological reservation', and it is precisely because of this that there is need for an
imperative to follow the indicative (cf. Rom. 6.1 f; Col. 3.1 f,
etc.). In other words, Paul's ethical stance is determined by his
sense of an eschatological tension between the 'Already' and the
'Not Yet'. Luke and the Pastor, on the other hand, appear to have

loosened the bond between ethics and eschatology. By the time he wrote Acts, at least, Luke no longer conceived of the end as imminent. And if there are traces of expectation of an imminent end in the Gospel, they do not appear to motivate his ethical teaching. That the end is certain, though not imminent, does act as one motivating force (Luke 17.20 f; 21.34 f; Acts 17.31) in the author's thought; and the same can be said of the Pastorals, for in 2 Tim. 4.1 f; Tit. 3.11 f, ethical exhortation is connected with allusions to the parousia. On the whole, however, it is clear that while both Luke and the Pastor believe firmly in a future parousia, it does not appear significantly to mould either the content or the tone of their ethical teaching. This is consonant with our earlier conclusion that eschatological beliefs are present, but not central, in Luke–Acts and the Pastorals.

Another contrast with Paul is that neither Luke nor the Pastor offers a theological or christological rationale for their ethical teaching. This point can best be illustrated by sketching a few of the theological themes which might have been (and frequently are in Paul) the basis for an ethic. For example, Paul views sin as both a demonic, personal force active in the universe and the universal condition of mankind (Rom. 5—7). Man is a fallen creature living in a fallen universe, and not simply one who performs immoral deeds. Neither Luke nor the Pastor reflects this radical sense of the sinfulness of man. In the Pastorals sin is understood as individual acts, the performance of immoral, and often observable, deeds (1 Tim. 5.24–5), which can in some cases be excused on the grounds of ignorance (1 Tim. 1.13). In Luke–Acts a similar view prevails: forgiveness is regularly described as the remission of sins (and not sin) (Luke 1.77; 24.17; Acts 2.38; 3.19; 5.31; 7.60; 10.43; 13.39; 22.16; 25.8; 26.18),[21] ignorance can be used as an excuse for sin (Luke 23.4; Acts 3.17; 13.27; 17.30), and in Luke 12.47 f it is suggested that ignorant sin leads to a lesser punishment. These individual acts of sin are occasionally linked with the influence of Satan (Acts 5.13; 26.18) but these are undeveloped, passing allusions. The notions of justification and faith, and the concept of a *theologia crucis* are, as we saw in the previous chapter, conceived of and used differently in Luke–Acts, the Pastorals, and Paul. Justification and faith, which might have formed the basis of a theological system in which ethics would have taken their place, are understood differently from Paul. The saving events of Christ's life are alluded to (cf. Acts 20.28; 2 Tim. 1.9 f; 2.8) but do not seem to affect the content or the proportion of the author's moral teaching.[22]

In place of an ethic rooted in a theology we have one based on common sense, pragmatism, and the natural order of things. In 1 Tim. 6.7 virtue, and in particular 'godliness with contentment', are recommended on the pragmatic grounds that as we brought nothing into this world, so we shall take nothing from it. In the light of this the pursuit of virtue and contentment and a simple life-style make good sense (vv. 8 f). Similarly, prayers for all in authority are motivated by the desire for a quiet and peaceable life (1 Tim. 2.2). The Pastor is also motivated by common sense, moderation, and a robust view of life. 1 Tim. 4.3–5 condemns both the forbidding of marriage and demands for abstention from foods; and while 1 Tim. 3.3, 8; Tit. 1.7; 2.3 warn against excessive consumption of wine, in 1 Tim. 5.23 Timothy is urged to use wine in moderation. The love of money is condemned (1 Tim. 6.9–10), but the rich can put their wealth to good use (1 Tim. 6.17–19). What appears to be a rationale for this stance is offered in 1 Tim. 4.3–5, where it is argued that 'everything created by God is good'. However, this is a solitary statement, aimed directly at the asceticism of the gnostic heretics, and is nowhere else used as the grounds for an ethic. Whatever is given in creation has still to be striven for; virtue is to be energetically pursued not passively received (2 Tim. 2.4–7; 1 Tim. 6.12).

Perhaps the most striking element in the 'natural' ethic of the Pastorals is the repeated quotation of catalogues of virtues and vices such as any good pagan would approve (1 Tim. 1.8 f; 3.1 f, 8 f; 2 Tim. 3.1 f; Tit. 1.5 f.; 2.1 f; 3.1 f). There is nothing especially Christian about either the virtues recommended or the motivation for pursuing them. They are good, because that is what society approves of. Two other themes emerge in connection with these lists. First, there is a noticeable concern about the impression Christians, especially Christian leaders, make on outsiders. They are to be virtuous both to impress their non-Christian neighbours and to avoid unnecessary slander being directed at the Church (1 Tim. 3.7; 6.1; Tit. 2.5; 3.8, 14), and this concern for the Church's reputation in the world is one of the clearest examples of the shift away from an eschatological perspective on ethics. Second, the Pastor tends to equate immorality with heresy and

morality with orthodoxy. The factious are, by definition, perverse
and sinful (Tit. 3.11) and virtue is exhibited in those who follow
the 'sound teaching' (1 Tim. 1.10; 2 Tim. 3.8–10; Tit. 1.9, 13;
2.1, 10). Right belief and right practice go hand in hand.

In Luke–Acts, as we have intimated already, we find far less
direct evidence for an overriding ethical concern. Even so, there
are sufficient indications that Luke shared the concerns of the
Pastor. His approval of virtue is indicated at several points. In
Luke 3.10–14, his summary of John the Baptist's preaching can
be paraphrased as, 'be good', 'be honest', 'be content', 'do not be
greedy'. In Luke 8.15, at the end of the interpretation of the
parable of the sower, the one who brings forth good fruit is the one
with 'an honest and good heart'. Joseph of Arimathea is described
as a 'good and righteous man' (Luke 23.50) and Barnabas as a
'good man' (Acts 11.24). Luke nowhere expands on what he means
by goodness, unless in the parable of the Good Samaritan (Luke
10.29–37), which exhorts others to do what Jesus himself did (cf.
Luke 6.1–11; 13.10–17; 14.1–6; 15.1 f): 'While Mark's Jesus
proclaims among sinful men the stark challenge of the Kingdom of
God, Luke's Jesus is the exemplar of generous and effective com-
passion for all in need'.[23]

There is also an interesting and specific point of connection.
H. Conzelmann has noted that one response of Luke to the delayed
parousia is to characterize the interim as a period requiring
endurance and patience (*hupomone*).[24] Luke adds a reference to
endurance in Luke 8.15 and emphasizes the theme in Luke 21.19.
Also he alone has the saying, 'You are those who have continued
with me in my trials; as my Father appointed a kingdom for me,
so do I appoint for you . . .' (Luke 22.28 f). It is significant perhaps
that 2 Tim. 2.12 contains the phrase, 'if we endure (*hupomenomen*)
we shall also reign with him', and that a similar use of *hupomone* is
found in 2 Tim. 2.10; 3.10.

The major difference between Luke and the Pastor is that the
former has a relatively small amount of distinctive ethical teaching.
In particular, there are parallels neither to the catalogues of vices
and virtues nor to the associated themes of the connection between
orthodoxy and morality and the reputation of the Church in
society. This might seem to be a serious difference. However, when
we take account of the difference in form, subject-matter and *Sitz
im Leben*, the differences become explicable. It is scarcely surpris-

ing, for example, to find no ethical exhortation and little ethical teaching in a narrative which gives, in broad outline, the progress of the Gospel throughout the world. It was not the author's purpose to concern himself with the detailed organization, belief, or morality of individual Christian communities. Conversely, it would be strange if such ethical material was absent from an epistle, especially an epistle addressed to communities plagued by a form of false teaching which had a direct influence on their ethical stance. It is true that we are given a fleeting glance of an identical situation in Acts 20.17 f, but then it seems that (at this stage) Luke did not see it as a serious problem. It was a threat which was visible on the horizon, but did not yet loom large. It does not seem to me, therefore, that these differences between Luke–Acts and the Pastorals are substantial. This opinion is reinforced by two further observations: first, that where his sources and subject-matter encourage him to develop a particular theme, the use of wealth for example, Luke is very close to the Pastorals; and second, while there are no catalogues of virtues in Luke–Acts, several of the individual terms within these catalogues do appear. It is to these last two points that we must now turn.

In their attitude towards the correct use of wealth Luke and the Pastor are in substantial agreement.[25] Moreover, it is significant that some of the material on this theme in the Pastorals finds its closest parallels in the special Lucan material in the Gospel. Obsession with money is seen as the source of both evil and stupidity in 1 Tim. 6.9–10, 17–19; Luke 12.16–21. In particular, the folly of hoarding wealth in this life is exposed and readers are urged to be 'rich towards God' (Luke 12.21) or 'rich in good deeds' (1 Tim. 6.18). Church leaders, to be qualified for office, must be 'not lovers of money' (*aphilarguros*) 1 Tim. 3.3; 2 Tim. 3.2; cf. Tit. 1.7). The same warning is found in Acts 20.33–5, in Paul's address to the Ephesian elders, though the terminology is not identical. The use of *philarguria* in conjunction with the charge 'not to be haughty' (*me hupselophronein*) in 1 Tim. 6.10, 17 finds its closest parallel in Luke 16.14–15, where Jesus calls the Pharisees 'lovers of money' (*philarguroi*) and condemns what is lofty (*hupselon*) among men as an abomination before God. Moreover, these are the only uses of *philarguros* in the New Testament. While both Luke and the Pastor are critical of the misuse of wealth, neither of them suggests that wealth is inherently evil. They both agree, for example, that the labourer is 'worthy of his reward' (*tou misthou autou* 1 Tim. 5.18; Luke 10.7 has the same phrase, whereas the Matthean version uses *tes trophes autou*). It is not the possession of money per se, but the meanness and greed which are often associated with it, which are condemned. Luke 3.10–14 condemns greed, and that is at least part of the message of Luke 16.19–31, while Luke 14.12–14; 19.1–10; Acts 20.35 recommend generosity. Luke seems to be more concerned to urge the generous, liberal use of wealth (as opposed to the miserly hoarding of it) than a forsaking of it in face of the coming Kingdom.[26] The same theme recurs in 1 Tim. 6.17–19 and in the emphasis on the virtue of hospitality (1 Tim. 3.2; 5.10; Tit. 1.8). Particularly striking is the similarity between the exhortation to the wealthy in 1 Tim. 6.18–19: 'to do good, to be rich in good deeds, liberal and generous, thus laying up for themselves a good foundation for the future, so that they may take hold of the life which is life indeed', and the obscure ending to the parable of the dishonest steward in Luke 16.9: 'And I tell you, make friends for yourselves by means of unrighteous mammon, so that when it fails they may receive you into the eternal habitations'. The interpretation of Luke 16.9 is, admittedly, difficult, but a common theme seems to underlie both passages: the generous and proper use of wealth now will increase one's credit in the life to come. The proper use of wealth is an implicit theme in Luke's references to the community of goods in the early Church (Acts 2.44–5; 4.34–7) and in the story of Ananias and Sapphira (Acts 5.1–11). The allusions to community of goods are of doubtful historicity, and it is improbable that Luke expected the Church of his day to follow the same procedure. It serves primarily as an illustration of the unity of the Church, yet at the same time the result is that the rich care for the poor and no one is left in need (Acts 4.34–5). It is for Luke a fine example of generosity and liberality.

We can now consider briefly the ethical terminology common to Luke and the Pastor. We have considered the terms 'faith' and 'righteousness' in the previous chapter. Suffice it here to say that both terms, though occasionally used in a manner which comes close to Pauline usage, are regularly used as ethical terms. In the Pastorals, for example, each of them can occur in lists of virtues as one virtue among others. Perhaps the most characteristic term in the Pastorals to summarize Christian behaviour is 'piety' (*eusebeia*) and its cognates. Of the twenty three occurrences in the New Testament fourteen are in the Pastorals, four in Luke, and six in 2 Peter. The term refers to a moral quality, a lifestyle and an attitude which are pleasing to God, but it is a vague term which has to be defined by its immediate context. 'Piety makes itself known in respectable conduct (1 Tim. 2.2; 5.4; 6.11; 2 Tim. 3.12; Tit. 2.12) such as is described in the *Haustafeln* (1 Tim. 2.8–15; Tit. 2.2–10). So it is the opposite of a former heathen life of vice (Tit. 3.3). It is the renunciation of 'irreligion' and 'worldly passions' (Tit. 2.12; 1 Tim. 6.9; 2 Tim. 2.22; 3.6; 4.3) yet it bears no traits of flight from the world, but is characterized by a 'sensibleness' (*sophrosune*) which avoids licentiousness and excess (1 Tim. 3.3, 8; Tit. 1.7; 2.3) and is frugal (1 Tim. 6.6–10). . . .'[27] It is a virtue in which one can train oneself (1 Tim. 4.7–8; 2.11), something to be striven for, and it is closely related to 'sound teaching' (1 Tim. 6.3; Tit. 1.1). Occasionally, it may even mean 'Christianity' (1 Tim. 3.16, possibly 1 Tim. 6.3; 2 Tim. 3.5), but generally the meaning follows Hellenistic usage—the appropriate human attitude towards god or gods. It is 'christianized' only insofar as it is specified that the deity is the Christian deity. The occurrences of 'piety' in Luke–Acts are few, but conform to the same pattern. In Acts 10.2, 7 it is used to describe Cornelius and a member of his staff, and it is clear, of course, that Luke approves highly of Cornelius, for it is because he is 'pious' and a friend of the Jews that he is singled out as the first Gentile to receive God's favour. Similarly, in Acts 17.23, it is used of non-Christians, describing their attitude toward 'the unknown god'. The context makes it clear that Luke approves of the Athenians' piety, even if he is vexed by their idolatry. Their idolatry may be misguided, an inadequate expression of their religious impulse, but the piety itself is laudable. In Acts 3.12 Peter and John claim that they have not performed a healing through their own power or piety (*eusebeia*) but through the miraculous power of God in Jesus. And the point surely is not to deny that the apostles are pious, but to deny that they can effect healing through their piety.[28] Luke, like the Pastor, uses 'piety' in its Hellenistic sense, and clearly it is something of which he approves.

Two more terms in the catalogues of the Pastorals occur in Luke–Acts. 'Self-control' is listed in Tit. 1.8 (cf. Gal. 5.23; 2 Pet. 1.6), and in Acts 24.25 is given some prominence as one of the main subjects of Paul's address to Felix and Drusilla. 'Prudence', or 'sobriety' (*sophron*), is mentioned nine times in the Pastorals and is used twice in Luke–Acts—once to describe a healed demoniac (Luke 8.35, cf. Mark 5.15), and once to describe the 'sober words' which Paul spoke to Festus (Acts 26.25). In neither case, however, is the reference to the virtue of 'prudence', but to the possession of reason or rationality as opposed to possession by a demon in the one case and to madness in the other.[29] More precise parallels to the usage in the Pastorals can be found in Rom. 12.3; 2 Cor. 5.13; 2 Pet. 4.7.

Finally, it is worth considering another phrase by which the Pastorals characterize Christian existence—having a 'good' or 'clean conscience' (*suneidesis agathe/kathara*). It is found in 1 Tim. 1.5, 18; 3.9; 2 Tim. 1.3, and its opposite is described as a 'corrupt' or 'seared conscience' (1 Tim. 4.1; Tit. 1.15). It is typical of post-Pauline usage for conscience to be qualified by adjectives such as good, clean, or bad, and in the Pastorals it has become a fixed expression. To have a good conscience is to be free from immoral behaviour and heretical beliefs. Certainly, 'good conscience' is associated with faith, but it is a particular, non-Pauline use of faith, so that there is no substantial connection with Paul: 'The term here implies the necessarily binding moral alternative, whereas in Paul it expresses the critical possibility of freedom in relation to the alternatives proposed'.[30] It is significant, therefore, that precisely the same terminology is found in Acts 23.1; 24.16 (cf. 1 Pet. 3.16, 21; Heb. 13.18). In both cases the phrase is used by Paul, but not in a Pauline way: 'I have lived before God in all good conscience up to this day' (23.1); 'I always take pains to have a clear conscience toward God and toward men' (24.16; contrast 1 Cor. 4.4). Particularly striking is the similarity to 2 Tim. 1.3: 'I thank God whom I serve with a clear conscience, as did my fathers . . .'.

To conclude, we have found considerable similarity in the attitude of Luke–Acts and the Pastorals towards the Christian's civic and ethical responsibilities. With respect to the Christian's attitude towards the State their message is the same. The general motivations for their ethical teaching seem to be identical and some specific ethical themes are found in both. There is nothing which contradicts the theory of common authorship and much to recommend it when allowance is made for the difference in purpose and subject-matter.

6
Church and Ministry

With regard to the nature of the Church, its officers and tradition, there is a remarkable similarity between Luke–Acts and the Pastorals. A. Strobel briefly mentions this, and it is worthwhile examining it in more detail.[1] A convenient place to begin is with the references to specific ecclesiastical offices, in particular elder, bishop, and deacon.

In the Pastorals 'elder' (*presbuteros*), which usually occurs in the plural, can mean 'old men' (1 Tim. 5.1; Tit. 2.2), and even in those passages where it clearly refers to an ecclesiastical functionary this sense is not entirely absent (1 Tim. 5.17; Tit. 1.5). We can glean several things about their responsibilities and privileges. 1 Tim. 5.17 states the following:

> Let the elders who rule well be considered worthy of double honour, especially those who labour in preaching and teaching.

It is implicit that the elders as a whole are the leaders of the community, but it is unlikely that he intends to present a hierarchical system with three or more grades; rather, he indicates that those among the group of elders who specialize or excel in certain duties (or simply spend more time at them) should receive a double stipend. It is, of course, axiomatic that all are paid something. The situation seems to be that while there is no formal hierarchy within the group of elders, some are emerging naturally as the more active and capable leaders. 1 Tim. 5.19–21 makes it clear that elders are to be disciplined if they persist in wrongdoing, but that they are to be protected from irresponsible accusations. In addition they are exhorted to blameless lives and to ensure that their family life does not bring disgrace upon the Church (Tit. 1.5–6). The over-riding concern of the Pastor is with the moral behaviour of the elders rather than with their specific ecclesiastical functions.

There is dispute over one function of the elders as described in

1 Tim. 4.14, where Timothy is exhorted as follows:

> Do not neglect the gift you have, which was given to you by
> prophetic utterance when the elders laid their hands upon you
> (*meta epitheseos ton cheiron tou presbuteriou*).

The final phrase is translated by some to mean, 'when you were
ordained into the office of elder'. It is urged that this interpretation
not only translates the Greek in line with a similar Jewish phrase
which refers to ordination (*semikhath zeqenim*), but also removes
the potential contradiction with 2 Tim. 1.6 where it is said that it
was Paul who laid hands on Timothy.[2] However, it is more probable that the RSV translation, 'when the elders laid their hands
upon you', is correct (i.e., treating it as a subjective genitive). The
parallels with the Semitic phrase are not especially close and do
not offer a compelling reason for interpreting the Greek as a
reference to ordination; and the tension between 1 Tim. 4.14 and
2 Tim. 1.6 can be explained either by the observation that they
reflect the formal differences between the two documents (1 Timothy is a congregational rule; 2 Timothy is an apostolic testament),
or by assuming that in neither case is the imposition of hands to be
seen as an unrepeatable act of ordination, in which case it could
have been performed more than once—though the reference to
'rekindling' the gift of God in 2 Tim. 1.6 might suggest a non-
repeatable action. This interpretation is moreover supported by
some other observations:[3] the similar phrase in 2 Tim. 1.6 is a
subjective genitive; there are no other references to Timothy as an
elder; and *presbuterion* almost always refers to a body of people
rather than an office. We can thus add to the list of elders' duties
the imposition of hands by which they consecrate individuals to
perform particular tasks of leadership.

Unlike the term elder, bishop (*episkopos*) is used only in the
singular in the Pastorals. As with the term 'elder', there are
examples of the titular use of the term outside the New Testament,
but since they do not describe any single role they shed only
indirect light on New Testament usage.[4] In the Pastorals there is
still some flexibility in the use of the term, since although it
unquestionably refers to an office in 1 Tim. 3.1, in Tit. 1.7 it
probably refers to a function. Thus while in Tit. 1.5 *presbuteros*
describes an office, in Tit. 1.7 *episkopos* describes a function, that
of overseeing, which is performed by at least some of these elders.[5]

The qualifications for a bishop/overseer are spelled out in 1 Tim. 3.1 f; Tit. 1.7 f and there is an overriding concern with their moral behaviour expressed in the conventional language of the catalogues of virtues and vices. The primary reason for demanding upright and sober behaviour from a bishop is the need to avoid unnecessary calumnies being directed at the Church by its opponents. The Church should at least be free from the charge that its leaders are immoral (1 Tim. 3.7). As to the duties of a bishop little is said except that they are to be good teachers (1 Tim. 3.2; Tit. 1.9) who faithfully transmit the 'sound teaching' and refute false teachers (Tit. 1.9 f).

The Pastorals make no clear distinction between elder and bishop. This is apparent in the description of their qualifications— e.g., both are to be 'blameless' (Tit. 3.6, 7), both are to 'rule', *prostenai* (1 Tim. 3.5; 5.17)—but it is not merely a matter of inference, since Tit. 3.5–7, and especially the connecting *gar* in v. 7, make it quite clear that elder and bishop refer to the same persons. Their precise relationship is unclear, and at least three possibilities come to mind. Elder and bishop could be completely synonymous, 'overseeing' being understood as a function of all elders. Alternatively, since bishop is always singular it has been argued that the Pastorals reflect a situation where the monarchical episcopate was well established. In each community there were several elders but one bishop—a specific office, whose incumbent was *primus inter pares*. Some think the monarchical system was in its infancy, while others argue for a more advanced stage of development.[6] A mediating position is to assume that while bishop and elder refer to the same office and the same people, 'bishop' singles out those who had special duties and responsibilities— perhaps those who 'presided well' or specialized in teaching and preaching (1 Tim. 5.17). Thus the situation was neither that all elders were overseers nor that only one elder could be bishop in any one community; rather, the bishops were the leading lights among the group of elders. The singular 'bishop' is then understood generically so that it does not imply only one bishop in each community.

Whichever interpretation is preferred, and the last seems most probable, we have no means of knowing how the two titles became combined. Paul does not refer to elders and only rarely refers to bishops and deacons (Phil. 1.1; Rom. 16.1). It is often suggested that originally elder and bishop were used in different Christian communities, but to describe approximately the same function— bishop in the Pauline churches and elder in the Jewish–Christian communities. If this was so, it is possible that the Pastor deliberately fuses the two terms, perhaps to avoid disputes about which was primary. But since there is no hint of dispute or polemic in the way the terms are used, it may simply be that he reflects the use current in his own communities.

The term deacon (*diakonos*) is used in conjunction with bishop (1 Tim. 3.8–13; cf. 3.1–7) but not with elder. Thus although the Pastor speaks of three offices or functions, they cannot be ranked into a threefold hierarchy. Like elder and bishop, the deacon is not yet a fixed technical term used exclusively for a church officer. It is used to describe an office in 1 Tim. 3.8–13, but in 1 Tim. 4.6 it is used in a non-technical way with reference to Timothy (cf. *diakonia*, 1 Tim. 1.12; 2 Tim. 4.5). As with bishops and elders the author tells us little or nothing about the duties of a deacon but much about the behaviour appropriate to the office. The requirements are not significantly different from those for a bishop; both they and their families are to lead blameless lives (1 Tim. 3.8–9, 12). Before taking office deacons are to be tested (1 Tim. 3.10), but we are not told how. 1 Tim. 3.11 probably refers to deaconesses (*gunaikes* is ambiguous and could refer to the wives of deacons) as in Rom. 16.1, though again we are informed only of the author's moral exhortations and not of their duties.

The use of the terms elder and bishop in Acts can conveniently be considered together since the only occurrence of bishop (*episkopos*) is in Acts 20.28 where it is implicitly equated with elder (*presbuteros*). In Acts elders appear in two main locations—in the Jerusalem church and the Pauline communities. In Acts 11.30; 15.1 f; 16.4; 21.18 they appear in Jerusalem but nothing is said of their origin, authorization, relationship to the apostles, or precise functions. They suddenly and mysteriously emerge on the Jerusalem scene in Acts 11.30 at roughly the same time as James (Acts 12.17). In Acts 11.30; 21.18 they are the representatives of the Jerusalem church and resemble a Jewish synagogue council, while in Acts 15—16 they are mentioned together with the apostles as the spokesmen of the Jerusalem church, and always in the phrase 'apostles and elders'. They no longer seem to be merely the representatives of the local Jerusalem church but act as part of an authoritative judicial body for the whole Church—more like the Jewish Sanhedrin than a local synagogue council.[7] That this is a function of circumstances and in no way specifically tied to the title 'elder' is proven by the other uses of elder in Acts 14.23; 20.17-38. The first of these passages mentions that Paul and Barnabas appointed elders in the communities they had founded. The setting is their imminent departure and, although we are not told directly of the elders' responsibilities, it is implied that they are to take the place of Paul and Barnabas as the guardians and leaders of the communities.

Acts 20.17 f indicates similar circumstances, though here the departure of Paul is final. As part of his farewell speech he predicts the problem that will face the church and exhorts the elders he is leaving in charge. It is implied that the elders have a crucial function in the post-apostolic era as guardians of apostolic tradition in the face of false teaching which will assault the church from within and without. At the same time Paul takes the opportunity to exhort the elders of Ephesus (who, we can be sure, are the paradigm for all elders in Pauline communities) to lead a moral life, especially in their attitude towards wealth. In these two respects there is only a loose connection with the Jerusalem elders. They too oppose false teachers, but their opponents were Judaizers and nothing is said of their ethical behaviour. A third mark of elders in Acts 20.17 f, also absent in the earlier references, is their role as overseers (*episkopoi*). As in the Pastorals, the equation of elder and bishop is presented casually, as a matter of course, and leaves us no clear idea of their precise relationship. H. von Campenhausen suggests that Luke may deliberately be introducing the older term (*episkopos*), current in Paul's day, and equating it with the newer term (*presbuteros*), with which he and his readers were more familiar.[8] Others suggest that Acts 20.28 reflects the early stages of the monarchical episcopate.[9]

Alternatively, we could interpret this passage merely as a reflection of the situation in Luke's day when elder and bishop were used to describe the same individuals. Luke would be indicating this in subtle fashion by fusing them in a speech which looks to the future—beyond the demise of Paul and the end of Acts, and towards the Church of his day.

The term 'deacon' (*diakonos*) does not occur in Luke–Acts. In Acts 6.1-6 we are told of the appointment of seven Hellenists to

'serve at tables' (v. 2) in order to free the Twelve to devote themselves to 'prayer and to the ministry of the word' (v. 4). Doubtless
Luke is not formally portraying the institution of the diaconate,
since 'serving at tables' is a specific job for a specific situation.
Moreover, it is not only the work of the Seven which is described
with the root *diakonia*, since the Twelve are to devote themselves
to prayer and 'the ministry of the word' (*te diakonia tou logou*).
Even so it is not impossible that Luke's readers, who were probably
familiar with the office of deacon, may have seen the incident as
marking the inauguration of this order.[10]

There are a few other terms we should consider which describe
special offices or functions in both Luke–Acts and the Pastorals.
Luke and the Pastor use the term 'evangelist' (*euaggelistes*) in an
official, if not a titular sense, of Philip in Acts 21.8 and Timothy in
2 Tim. 4.5. More important are the references to Christian prophets who work in conjunction with the more formal officers. The
Pastorals refer to them as follows:

> This charge I commit to you, Timothy, my son, in accordance
> with the prophetic utterances which pointed to you, that
> inspired by them you may wage the good warfare (1 Tim. 1.18).

> Do not neglect the gift you have, which was given you by
> prophetic utterance when the elders laid their hands on you
> (1 Tim. 4.14).

The primary role of prophets in both cases is to single out future
leaders of the community. The selection itself, together with the
ensuing consecration, is viewed as a source of inspiration and
strength in the fulfilment of official duties. In Acts prophetic
figures also play an active role in the life of Christian communities:
Agabus prophesies famine (Acts 11.27 f), Judas and Silas are sent
by the Jerusalem church to accompany Paul and Barnabas in the
dissemination of the apostolic decree (Acts 15.22–32), Philip's
four daughters are prophetesses (Acts 21.9), and Agabus prophesies
Paul's fate (Acts 21.10–11). Above all, however, the role of
prophets in the Pastorals is paralleled in Acts 13.1–3:

> Now in the church at Antioch there were prophets and teachers,
> Barnabas, Symeon who was called Niger, Lucius of Cyrene,
> Manaen a member of the court of Herod the tetrarch, and Saul.

While they were worshipping the Lord and fasting, the Holy Spirit said, 'Set apart for me Barnabas and Saul for the work to which I have called them'. Then after fasting and praying they aid their hands on them and sent them off.

The prophets and teachers, under the inspiration of the Spirit, single out Paul and Barnabas for their divinely-appointed task and, before sending them off, lay their hands upon them. The parallel with 1 Timothy is remarkable.

The reference to the imposition of hands points to another theme common to Luke and the Pastor. In Acts it is used in a variety of situations. In Acts 6.6; 13.3, it accompanies the selection and dedication of individuals for a specific task. In Acts 19.6 Paul baptizes and lays hands on Ephesian disciples who have known only the baptism of John, and they immediately receive the Spirit, speak in tongues, and prophesy. Acts 8.17 also connects this rite with the gifts of the Spirit, but on this occasion the recipients have already been baptized. The imposition of hands thus has no fixed role to play. It can accompany official dedication to a particular task, but does not always do so (Acts 1.15 f; 14.23 f; 15.40); and it can be associated with the gift of the Spirit, but is not always so (Acts 8.17; 19.6). In the Pastorals the ceremony is associated most closely with a solemn dedication to a particular task. 1 Tim. 4.14 and 2 Tim. 1.6 speak of the gift (*charisma*) which Timothy received at the laying on of hands by the elders or by Paul. The injunction in 1 Tim. 5.22—'Do not be hasty in the laying on of hands, nor participate in another man's sins'—can be understood in the same way, i.e., as a reference to a form of ordination into an office. Timothy is warned to avoid hasty ordination, lest he appoint an unworthy elder.[11] Alternatively, it could be a reference to a ceremony of reconciliation following the disciplining of a member of the community.[12] Whereas the former interpretation involves assuming a close connection between v. 21 and the preceding material, the latter sees it as beginning a new section. There are no other allusions to a ceremony of reconciliation in the New Testament, and this speaks against the latter view, but in its favour is that it more readily explains the injunction not to 'participate in the sins of others'. If it is accepted it would indicate that the Pastorals do not have a single concept of the imposition of hands.

At this stage it is perhaps worthwhile to summarize the similarities observed so far:

1　Both Luke and the Pastor mention the two major offices/ functions of bishop and elder, and in this respect they stand alone in the New Testament. The contrast with Paul is noteworthy, since he nowhere mentions elders. The Pastor adds a third office, that of deacon; Luke does not, though one part of his narrative may have been interpreted as an allusion to deacons.

2　Even more striking, both Luke and the Pastor equate elders and bishops by using them to describe the same individuals. It is not clear in either case what the precise interrelationship is, but it may well have been the same in both instances. Similarly, although in the Pastorals deacons are not equated with elder-bishops, there is no clear hierarchical structure and the qualifications for the one office are no different from those for the other.

3　Neither Luke nor the Pastor provides a detailed description of the tasks of the various officials. However, with respect to elder-bishops there are some indications that they envisage similar functions. In Acts 20, the only place where Luke specifically broaches the topic, two points are emphasized: first, the primary role of elder-bishops is to defend the Church against false teachers and hold fast to the true Pauline teaching; secondly, Luke's concern for the moral behaviour of these leaders is illustrated in the advice about the proper attitude to wealth. The same two points are emphasized, in greater detail, in the Pastorals. Indeed, it is characteristic of the Pastorals that they tell us virtually nothing about the formal duties of church officials but are obsessed with their moral conduct and their transmission of apostolic tradition; though this may in part be because the duties were common knowledge to writer and readers.

4　With respect to the role of Christian prophets and the ceremony of the laying on of hands, Luke–Acts and the Pastorals are remarkably similar. In many ways the narratives of Acts provide the best illustration of the statements in the Pastorals.

5　Two minor points: both authors refer to the office of evangelist; and while Luke has no parallel to the order of widows (1 Tim. 5.3–16), unless this is indicated in the description of Anna (Luke

2.36–8), care for widows (Acts 6.1 f) and awareness of them as a distinct group (Acts 9.39 f) are referred to in Acts.

So far the discussion has been limited to a comparison of specific ecclesiastical titles and functions. Our task is now to consider the broader problem of the concept of the Church.

In neither Luke–Acts nor the Pastorals is there a rigid concept of office or of church order. Indeed, the very concept of 'order' may be anachronistic as far as Acts is concerned.[13] In Acts there is no clear definition of the duties of elders, nor is there an explanation of their relationship to apostles. They appear without warning in Acts 11.30 within a community which up to that point has been dominated by the apostles, and in Acts 15—16 they are presented as co-leaders of the Jerusalem church. When we are told of the appointment of elders, it is by Paul and Barnabas and not the Twelve (Acts 14.23). In the one place where the role of elders is discussed, they are identified with bishops and their selection for this role is expressly attributed to the Spirit (Acts 20.28; cf. 6.3–5; 13.1–3). Prophets, evangelists, and teachers are also mentioned, but no attempt is made to integrate them, together with the apostles and elders, into an ecclesiastical structure. Moreover, not all the important figures bear titles. Paul and Barnabas are only twice called apostles (Acts 14.4, 14) and Silas and Timothy, as well as other Pauline aides, have no official rank. Thus E. Schweizer correctly concludes: 'This almost casual mention of special office-bearers in the Church and the absence of definite titles, show that the order of these forms of service is not fundamental to the Lukan church'.[14]

A similar lack of rigidity is found in the Pastorals. Paul is the only apostle mentioned, and both the content and format of the letters assert his authority. At the same time we are not told of any form of ecclesiastical succession from Paul to the bishops, elders, and deacons. In addition, these three terms fluctuate between a technical and non-technical usage, describe overlapping roles, and cannot be ranked into a hierarchical system. And, as in Acts, there are important individuals, such as Timothy and Titus, who bear no official title, and other figures such as prophets and evangelists who function alongside the other officers. In the Pastorals an office is still seen primarily as a 'ministry', but there is a noticeable interest in the qualifications for, and responsibilities and rewards of, leadership.[15] When commissioned to a particular office or role, individuals can expect special gifts; indeed, the very act of commissioning or ordination can be a strength and support (1 Tim. 4.14; 2 Tim. 1.6). On the other hand church officials are not infallible, for they can sin and fall short in their appointed role. Timothy is exhorted to hold on to and rekindle the gift of God (1 Tim. 1.18; 2 Tim. 1.6) which implies that he could fail in this task. Paul's supporters can turn sour (2 Tim. 4.10), and Hymenaeus and Alexander make such a 'shipwreck of their faith' that they are delivered to Satan (1 Tim. 1.19–20). Presumably these two were prominent members of the community and possibly even office-bearers. On viewing the Pastorals from a different perspective, the same result emerges. Unlike Ignatius or Clement, the Pastor does not claim that a particular church order has divine sanction. Of course we must assume that he believed God approves of officers and organization, but he nowhere ties a particular understanding of office or hierarchy to the divine will. In the Pastorals the importance and authority of church offices are ultimately secondary to the 'sound teaching', the apostolic tradition. It is this which provides the rationale for the existence of offices, for it is to the preservation and dissemination of sound teaching that church leaders are committed.

The concepts of tradition and succession are also similar in Luke–Acts and the Pastorals. The superficial impression given by Acts might be that the twelve apostles control the Church. Certainly, they are the central authority in the early chapters of Acts: they check significant new developments (Acts 8.14; 9.26 f; 11.1 f, 22), and they host the crucial discussions about the Gentile mission (Acts 15.1 f; 16.4). However, while Luke may prepare the way for the idea of a central government of the Church by the Twelve and an orderly, continuous line of succession from them, that is not his own view. Indeed it is remarkable that, while Luke has so much to say about the activities of the Twelve and clearly indicates that they had an important role, he has no concept of apostolic succession. Elders appear in Jerusalem alongside the Twelve, but with no hint that they were commissioned by them (Acts 11.30; 15.1 f); and when the Twelve disappear, the elders and James are left in control (Acts 21.18 f). On the whole Paul works independently of the Jerusalem church, though not without its approval. When he appoints elders (Acts 14.23) there is no suggestion that he first had to be authorized by the Twelve in order to legitimize his appointments. If Luke had had such a rigid concept of apostolic succession it is difficult to see how he could portray Barnabas as the apostolic delegate who examines and approves the work at Antioch (Acts 11.22 f) and yet as a man who is subsequently singled out and commissioned for missionary work by the prophets and teachers of that same community (Acts 20.17 f). It is important that the elders in Pauline churches be instructed by and remain faithful to the teaching of Paul (Acts 20.17 f), but it is not said that this function is tied to a particular office in an ecclesiastical line of tradition. Luke is not interested in a concept of succession in any formal sense, nor in a single, unbroken line stretching back to the Twelve. In different circumstances, different individuals take the lead: the Twelve in Jerusalem, prophets and teachers in Antioch, and Paul in the mission field. Naturally things are not wholly haphazard. As a rule, leaders are installed with prayer, fasting, and the laying-on of hands, and they in turn can commission others (Acts 6.1 f; 13.2–3; 14.23 f; 15.40). As von Campenhausen succinctly puts it:

> This, however, does not depend on particular valid forms, nor on a link with particular people who happen to be lawfully consecrated. The connection is inward and spiritual, and the continuity concrete and historical, not merely sacramental or juristic . . . this way of thinking about the matter is continued in the Pastoral Epistles, which theologically are close to Luke.[16]

To this we can add that, while there is no rigid concept of apostolic succession, in the one passage that explicitly looks beyond the first generation there is a concern for the preservation of Pauline and apostolic tradition. Paul is preparing the Ephesian elders for his departure (Acts 20.17 f) and, while it is not explicitly said that they should adhere to his teaching, the overall format of the speech and the references to Paul's previous declaration to them of 'the whole counsel of God' (vv. 27, 31) imply much the same thing.

E. Käsemann has suggested that one mark of Luke's 'Early Catholicism' is his insistence on the *Una Sancta Catholica*, i.e., that the Church is the sole source of authority and salvation and that any deviants must either be absorbed or stand condemned.[17] His view is based primarily on Acts 19.1–7, when the disciples of John the Baptist are brought into the Church by baptism, the laying-on of hands, and the gift of the Spirit. Taken in isolation this incident lends some credibility to Käsemann's view, but it would be unfair to characterize the whole of Acts by this one story. Our earlier observations about the elders, apostles, Paul and his companions, serve as a necessary counterbalance. Insofar as Luke would have agreed that salvation was to be found in the Church, it was not because he saw the Church as a hierarchically-ordered *Heilsanstalt*, but 'because he knows that it is in the context of the Church that the saving word must be heard and believed and because it does not occur to him that any sincere believer would wish to separate himself from those to whom he owed it'.[18] Moreover, when the problem of gnostic heresy is briefly touched upon (Acts 20.29 f) it is neither defined nor countered in terms of an orthodox Church being assaulted from outside by heretical teachers, since the problem is as much internal as external (vv. 29–30). The response to false teaching is not in terms of ecclesiology but in terms of the preservation of Pauline, apostolic tradition.

In the Pastorals tradition and succession are similarly inter-related. Paul, as the ostensible author of the letters, and Timothy and Titus as the recipients, stand in a unique position. And yet there is no clear line of succession from Paul to Timothy and Titus, to the elder-bishops and to the deacons. Titus is instructed to appoint elders in every town (Tit. 1.5) and Timothy is advised to entrust what he hears from Paul 'to faithful men who will be able to teach others also' (2 Tim. 2.2). In the latter case, however, nothing is said about ordination or an office. As with Acts, it would have been possible for someone to have looked back from a more developed ecclesiastical situation and claim the Pastorals as the paradigm for his own day, but this would not accurately convey the intention of the author. There is no theory of succession as a fixed, canonical principle. If the author had been intent on presenting a sacramental link between Paul and his successors he would scarcely have retained both references to the imposition of hands on Timothy, the one by Paul (2 Tim. 1.6) and the other by the elders (1 Tim. 4.14). The connection between Paul and his aides, like the concept of office in general, is not understood sacramentally, as a form of apostolic succession; rather it is understood in terms of the preservation of apostolic tradition. It is true that Timothy and Titus have a somewhat ambivalent role, since neither is given a title and their precise relationship with other church officials is unclear. This is probably because the author uses them as part of the dramatic setting of the epistles and because he presents them more as ideal types of the Christian minister than as real historical personages. The real addressees are Christian communities and, in particular, their leaders. Timothy and Titus are the media by which the author presents his message. Their primary role is to be the true bearers of Pauline tradition, which they neither reformulate nor reinterpret, but simply transmit.[19] They are the figures who guarantee that the teaching of the epistles (and not the gnostic versions) correctly preserves Pauline tradition. As in Acts, it is clear that the noblest task of a church official is to guard the apostolic tradition. This defines the essential feature of the Church and its leaders (1 Tim. 1.10; 4.1, 6, 13; 5.17; 6.3, 20; 2 Tim. 2.14–16, 23; 3.10; 4.3; Tit. 1.9, 14; 2.1; 3.9 f). Although the concept of office is important in the Pastorals, it is ultimately secondary to the apostolic tradition, for it is the latter which forms the basis of and rationale for the former.

The depiction of the Church as an institution and its response to heresy are very similar to Acts. The Church is described as 'the household of God', 'the pillar and bulwark of the truth'; but it is not implied that it is an institution free from heresy. The problem is clearly as much internal as external (1 Tim. 1.19–20; 2 Tim. 2.17 f) as was foreseen in Acts. The Church is a mixed group containing noble and ignoble vessels (2 Tim. 2.20 f) and only the 'Lord knows those who are his' (2 Tim. 2.19). The response to this situation is insistence on the teaching of Paul, on the preservation of apostolic tradition and sound teaching. Apostolic tradition is the author's yardstick. As in Acts, so in the Pastorals the boundary between true and false teaching, orthodoxy and heresy, is not the boundary between the Church and the world but the boundary between those who know and preserve the tradition and those who deviate from it. One can infer from the Pastorals as from Acts, that the author believes that salvation lies within the Church for it is there that the 'sound teaching' is preserved. But this belief is never elevated into a fixed, canonical principle. Finally, it is worth noting that the Pastorals, like Acts but unlike Paul, do not engage in a dialogue with their opponents, exploring the areas of disagreement and searching for common ground or mutually acceptable expressions of belief. Their approach is unsubtle. False teaching is met head on with blunt contradiction which recalls believers to the sound apostolic teaching and which, by definition, condemns all who stand outside it.

The sole example of disciplinary action mentioned in Acts is the story of Ananias and Sapphira (Acts 5.1–10). This curious story is only indirectly related to the theme of church discipline, since its primary purpose is to emphasize the purity of the Church and the miraculous power of the apostles. It should not, therefore, be pressed to yield juristic information.[20] In the Pastorals the attitude towards deviants is varied. In Tit. 1.13; 3.10 Titus is urged to rebuke them sharply and, if that fails, to have no more to do with them. Public rebuke is also envisaged in 1 Tim. 5.20 for persistent sinners. In 1 Tim. 1.19–20 a more severe treatment is envisaged: Paul delivers them 'to Satan, that they may learn not to blaspheme' (cf. 2 Tim. 2.17; 4.14). That the punishment is intended to be educative implies that it is not irrevocable, as it was for example in 1 Cor. 5.5 (though this was also aimed ultimately at salvation). In this respect Luke and Paul agree more closely. Also, in the Pastorals one can detect the beginnings of a disciplinary system aimed at reforming and rehabilitating deviants and yet, as in Acts, the notion of a special and miraculous apostolic intervention is still present.

It is already clear that there is remarkable similarity between Luke and the Pastor with respect to church order. Before we summarize the evidence, however, we can briefly consider the differences that have been noted. Perhaps the most obvious is the tendency of Luke to identify the title 'apostle' with the Twelve, whereas the Pastor uses it solely of Paul, and we shall offer an explanation for this in chapter nine. E. Schweizer claims that the Pastorals have lost the Lucan (and Matthean) concept of *Heilsgeschichte*: 'The Church no longer regards itself as a developing factor, essentially determined by its own history. It feels its own existence much more strongly as a static one; it has established itself firmly and is now concerned to hold on to what has been obtained, and to remain as it is'.[21] However it seems to me that this difference is more apparent than real. The sense of *Heils-*

geschichte in Luke, the notion of the Church as a dynamic, ever-expanding entity but with its roots firmly in the past, is in large part the result of the subject-matter of Acts. It *is* the story of the expansion of the Church from Jerusalem to the 'ends of the earth', and as such could scarcely portray the Church as anything but a constantly evolving organism. As an ostensibly historical narrative about the history of the Church a *heilsgeschichtliche* perspective, in Schweizer's sense, is almost inevitable. Moreover, when Luke does glance beyond the ending of Acts and the demise of Paul, he also envisages a period of retrenchment, a holding fast to the received apostolic tradition (Acts 20.17 f). The Pastorals, on the other hand, are written in a different genre and for a different purpose. In a situation where gnostic teachers were claiming Paul as the authority for their teaching and using the Old Testament as the basis of their speculations, it would have been irrelevant to recount the history of the Church up to and including Paul or to produce a *heilsgechichtliche* scheme. The urgent need was to counter false teaching and, in particular, the misuse of Paul; and this is effected by epistles written in Paul's name.

A further difference is pointed out by H. von Campenhausen,[22] when he says that the Pastorals give the impression of a slightly more organized church life than Acts. The concept of office is more developed and less patriarchal than in Acts; there are clear references to different types of office (elder-bishops and deacons); and there are initial signs of a developing disciplinary system. In addition, he notes, the activities of the false teachers, which merit no more than a passing allusion in Acts, are far more obvious in the Pastorals. The latter confirms my view that when Luke wrote Acts the gnostics had begun their activities, but that when he wrote the Pastorals their influence had greatly increased and they posed a serious threat. The development in ecclesiastical organization could be explained in two ways. First, since Acts ostensibly describes the early period of the Church one might argue that the less developed ecclesiastical system accurately reflects the situation in the early Church. Second and more likely however is that, insofar as Acts reflects the situation of Luke's day, the more developed situation in the Pastorals represents the actual development in the interim—a development which would have occurred naturally in the course of time, but which was no doubt hastened by the increasing gnostic threat.

We can now draw together our conclusions:

1   As our earlier summary indicated, Luke and the Pastor refer mostly to the same offices—elder, bishop, evangelist, prophets—and in the same way.

2   They have a similar view of the laying-on of hands and its significance for Christian leaders.

3   Their concepts of tradition and succession are the same. In both the former is more important than the latter.

4   Their concept of the relationship between the Church and salvation, and the definition of and reaction to heresy, is similar.

5   They both base their instructions to church leaders for the post-apostolic era on the prophetic foresight of the departing Paul.

6   The shifts of emphasis that can be observed are slight and wholly explicable when account is taken of the different situations at the time of writing.

One explanation of these similarities would be that they are fortuitous. They reflect a situation which was fairly widespread and it is no more than coincidence that two writers should present such a similar understanding of the Church. This is not impossible. I would argue, however, that they are there because the same man wrote both Luke–Acts and the Pastorals, and that what he began in the one he developed in the other.

7
Christology

Much discussion of the christology of Luke–Acts is concerned inevitably with the question how accurately Luke portrays the beliefs and preaching of the early Church. The broad conclusions of this debate are significant for our discussion, in that it will be argued below that Luke characteristically uses diverse, and often ancient, christological materials without integrating them into any overall scheme. But having concluded that certain concepts are pre-Lucan, we shall not need to discuss their assignation to a specific layer of early Christian tradition.[1]

Hans Conzelmann correctly observes that 'the special elements in Luke's christology cannot be set out by statistical analysis of the titles applied to Jesus', for his use of them is promiscuous and often without reference to their original meaning.[2] It is important, moreover, to consider the overall structure of the two volumes, bearing in mind both the immediate impression that would be made on Luke's audience and the alterations Luke makes to his sources.[3] Nor should it be overlooked that in the speeches of Acts, at least, the emphasis is more on christological events than on christological titles.[4] Conzelmann's judgement needs to be qualified only to the degree that the numerical dominance of *kurios* as a title in Luke–Acts *is* indicative of Luke's concentration on the exalted Jesus as his major christological theme.

The consensus is that the christology of Luke–Acts is fundamentally an exaltation christology. The most cursory glance through Luke–Acts confirms that this is so—from the prefigurement of the ascension in the Gospel, through the two pivotal narratives of the ascension in Luke 24 and Acts 1, to the emphasis on the resurrection and exaltation in the speeches of Acts.

Many distinctive Lucan features contribute to this picture. To Mark he has added the birth narratives (Luke 1—2), the programmatic preview of his ministry (Luke 4.16 f), the journey to

Jerusalem (Luke 9.51; 19.46) and the ascension narratives (Luke 24.49 f; Acts 1.9–11), and it is especially in these innovations that his viewpoint emerges. Thus *poreuomai* (Luke 4.30) may anticipate the death (Luke 9.51; 22.22, 33) and ascension (Acts 1.10–11) of Jesus,[5] while the addition of *exodos* in Luke 9.31 and the use of *analempsis* in Luke 9.51 (cf. Acts 1.11, 22) clearly allude to the ascension.[6] In Luke's view the whole of Jesus' earthly career, especially the post-transfiguration period, anticipates and comes to a climax in the ascension. It is true that there is a developing awareness after the transfiguration of the necessity of Jesus' suffering and death (Luke 9.22, 44; 12.50; 13.32–5; 19.31–3),[7] but not as an end in itself. It is but one stage on the path to glory.

The Lucan resurrection stories contain several distinctive emphases: the physicality of Jesus' resurrected form (Luke 24.3, 22–3, 36 f; cf. Luke 23.55; Acts 10.41; 13.31), the necessity of Jesus' suffering to fulfil both scripture (Luke 24.26, 44–6) and his own predictions (Luke 24.6–7, 44), and the concentration on Jerusalem as the exclusive centre of action (Luke 24.6, 46–9; Acts 1.1–8). The result is a coherent, often distinctive, account in which 'the resurrection is not an act in itself or a symbol of exaltation or parousia, but a point of transition'.[8] In the orderly succession of events Jesus' death, resurrection and ascension, and the gift of the Spirit each have their role; but among them, the ascension is supreme.

Luke's narratives of the ascension (Luke 24.50–3; Acts 1.9–11) are unique, but not wholly in accord with each other. Among the host of problems this raises we need concentrate only on the christological implications.[9] That Luke presents two accounts of the ascension is in itself significant, for what Luke considers to be important, he repeats. By making them the mid-point of his two-volume work, Luke may be using a literary convention in order to emphasize their importance,[10] though in an ostensibly chronological account they could scarcely have been placed anywhere else. That the ascension is the climax of Jesus' earthly life is clear not only from its position at the end of the Gospel but from the allusions to it earlier in the narrative. The disciples' joyous worship sets an appropriate tone, since they are responding no longer to the earthly Jesus but to the glorified Lord. It is in this light that his earthly career, especially his suffering and ignominious death, must now be viewed.

Acts 1.9–11 is different in tone and emphasis. The event itself is less important than the disciples' response to it—a response not of worshipful joy, but of doubt and perplexity.[11] Their concern that this may be their last view of Jesus is allayed by the angelic reassurance that he will return in the same manner in which he has departed (v. 11). But their attention is drawn away from this event to the coming of the Spirit and the universal proclamation, the essential presupposition for which is the exaltation of Jesus (Luke 24.47 f; Acts 1.6–8; 2.33). Jesus' parousia is not denied, but is overshadowed by his present lordship.[12] The exaltation is thus not only the triumphant conclusion to his earthly life, but the essential precondition for the expansion of his Church.

In the speeches of Acts the resurrection and exaltation are central components of the kerygma.[13] The resurrection is described by *anistanai* (Acts 2.24, 32; 13.33 f; 17.31) or the more traditional *egeiren* (Acts 3.15; 4.10; 5.30; 10.40; 13.30, 47), but in both cases the stress is on the action of God rather than of Jesus. The same is probably true of the occasional use of the intransitive *anastenai* (Luke 18.33; 24.7, 46; Acts 10.41; 17.3). Here, as in the references to exaltation (Acts 2.32–3; 5.31; cf. *analemphthe* Acts 1.2, 11, 22), Jesus' role is passive and subordinate, so that even the climax of his career is seen as an act of God. That resurrection and exaltation fulfil the promises of Scripture is a traditional theme willingly taken up by Luke (Luke 18.31; 24.25 f, 44–6; cf. 1 Cor. 15.3 f), as is the specific use of Ps. 110 (Acts 5.31); but the use of Ps. 16.8–11 (Acts 2.25 f; 13.35 f) and the emphasis on apostolic witness to these events (Acts 2.32; 3.15; 5.32; 10.41; 13.31) are distinctive Lucan emphases.

It has been suggested that some speeches amalgamate the resurrection and exaltation (Acts 2.32–3; 5.30–1; cf. Luke 24.1 f) in a manner inconsistent with their clear separation in Acts 1.[14] In Acts 2.32–3 the association of resurrection with 'witness' and the ascension with the 'Spirit' might seem to distinguish them, though the shift from the one to the other is almost imperceptible (cf. *oun* v. 33). Acts 5.30–1 mentions them separately, but not necessarily as two separate events. In the light of Acts 1.1 f it could be argued that their identification is only apparent and results from the brevity of the kerygmatic outline,[15] but if Luke 24.1 f is taken as an analogy (though it is also vague) the opposite conclusion could be reached. If the latter, then they are presumably traditional statements which Luke understood in the light of Acts 1, but whose original meaning was rather different.

Among Lucan christological titles *kurios* is unmistakably his favourite. *kurios/kurie* occur some 204 times in Luke–Acts, of which approximately half refer to Jesus (31 of these are the vocative *kurie*). Jesus, as *kurios*, is seen as the content or object of faith in connection with *pisteuein/pistis* (Acts 11.17; 16.31; 20.21; cf. 5.14; 9.42; 16.15; 18.8), *didache/didaskein* (Acts 13.12; 28.31), *euaggelizesthai* (Acts 11.20) and *marturion* (Acts 4.33). It is used otherwise in narrative settings, of which the fifteen occurring only in the Gospel of Luke are particularly noteworthy.

The ease and familiarity with which Luke uses *kurios* of Jesus indicate that it was for him the designation which most naturally sprang to mind. This might suggest in turn that he did not carefully distinguish between the use of it for the earthly and the resurrected Jesus—a view which C. F. D. Moule, however, has challenged.[16] He observes that while Elizabeth and Zechariah, in a moment of prophetic insight, call Jesus 'Lord' (Luke 1.43, 76), and angels (Luke 2.11) and Christ himself (Luke 19.31) can do the same, prior to the resurrection his disciples and followers do not address him so. For apart from these passages *kurios* occurs only in Luke's editorial sections where he, as the author, calls Jesus 'Lord'. The vocative *kurie*, he argues, is no more than a respectful form of address. After the resurrection there is a noticeable change, for now Jesus' disciples freely call him 'Lord' (cf. Luke 24.34, etc.). Moule admits that this does not prove that Luke avoided anachronism or that his reconstruction is accurate. Nevertheless, he thinks the pattern is deliberate. Luke accurately reflects the fact that the early Church did not use *kurios* in its full christological sense until after the resurrection.

It is probable, however, that more weight must be given to the casual, editorial use of *kurios* in the Gospel and for the following reasons.[17] First, *kurios* is by its very nature either an affirmation of faith by those who share a common conviction (Luke 1.43, 45; 24.34; Acts 8.22) or a proclamation to non-believers (e.g., Acts 2.36; 10.36), and neither situation arises naturally in the Gospel. The absence of *kurios* in the non-editorial sections of the Gospel is probably, therefore, fortuitous. Second, the vocative *kurie* often comes close to the full meaning of *kurios*, especially in passages where they are closely connected (Luke 10.1, 17; 10.39, 41;

12.41, 42; 17.5, 37; 19.8a, 8b; 22.33, 61; and cf. Acts 9.5, 13 with 9.1, 10, 15). F. Hahn comments that 'a certain development of the term is observable in him (Luke) inasmuch as it is placed in emphatic relation to the absolute *kurios* applied to the earthly Jesus'.[18] Luke's use of *kurios* thus appears to be both indiscriminate and anachronistic, since he believed it to be an appropriate designation from the announcement of Jesus' birth onwards. Apparently it is for Luke *the* appropriate way to address Jesus, the exact connotation varying with circumstances. It could be no more than the familiar designation used casually by Christians; in devotional contexts it carried greater weight; and in formal statements of belief such as creeds and sermons it could have universal, even cosmic, connotations.

Even though he uses *kurios* of the earthly Jesus it is unquestionably Luke's primary designation for the exalted Jesus too. It is possible that *kurios* was used originally in connection with the parousia (cf. 1 Cor. 16.22; *Did.* 10.6) and that this is reflected in Luke 6.46; 7.21; 13.25–6;[19] but if so, this is no longer important for Luke. If the attribution of *kurios* to the exalted Jesus was a subsequent move, it was a very early shift of which Luke would have been unaware. The free interchange of *kurios* between God and Jesus, so that we are often unsure to whom it refers, apparently does not imply an equal status for Jesus, though doubtless it encouraged the development of such a notion in subsequent years.

Christos, the next most common designation for Jesus, occurs twelve times in the Gospel, always in the technical sense of 'Messiah' (Luke 2.11, 26; 3.15; 4.41; 9.20; 20.41; 22.67; 23.2, 35, 39; 24.36, 46). The same is true of sixteen of the occurrences in Acts (Acts 2.31, 36; 3.18, 20; 4.26, 33; 5.42; 8.5, 37; 9.22; 10.36; 17.3 twice; 18.5, 28; 26.23) while the remaining twelve are used simply as a proper name (Acts 2.38; 3.6; 4.10; 8.12; 9.34; 10.48; 11.17; 16.18; 20.21; 24.24; 28.31); though the distinction is not always clear (e.g., Acts 9.34). H. J. Cadbury's claim that 'for this writer it is not a proper name'[20] is thus an exaggeration, though there are only two examples of the simple form 'Jesus Christ' (9.34; 24.24), the remainder appearing in fixed phrases such as 'the name of Jesus Christ' or 'Lord Jesus Christ'. Peculiar to Luke are the related phrases 'his Christ' (Acts 3.18; cf. 4.6), 'Lord's Christ' (Luke 2.26; 2.11, *v.l.*) and 'the Christ of God' (Luke 9.20; 23.25) which both reflect the original Jewish notion of Messiahship and indicate Luke's subordinationist view of Jesus.

When Luke wrote, the titular use of *christos* would have had an archaic ring. But it always occurs in apologetic contexts and normally when Jews are being addressed, for both the Samaritans and Agrippa, the apparent exceptions (Acts 8.5; 26.23), had some knowledge of Jewish belief.[21] In context the titular uses of *christos* are thus entirely appropriate. They are probably an accurate reflection of a central theme in early Christian preaching, for even if Jesusr efused the label *christos* and early believers did not immediately turn to it as a category appropriate to their understanding of Jesus, it would not have been long after the resurrection that some discussion of the Messianic category would have been forced upon them. They were, after all, preaching to fellow-Jews, and Jesus had been crucified as a messianic pretender.[22]

The obvious stumbling block in the identification of Jesus with Messiah, i.e. his suffering and death, was explained at an early date by reference to Scripture (1 Cor. 15.3–5). Luke pays special attention to this (Luke 24.26, 46; Acts 3.18; 17.3; 26.23), but although the precise wording and emphasis may be his own, the theme itself is traditional. Luke was probably influenced by events in his own day too,[23] for doubtless the same issues were debated then (cf. Justin's *Dialogue with Trypho*), but he has certainly not anachronistically located them in early Christian preaching.

Two uses of *christos* stand out. Acts 3.19–20 is almost the only evidence for the view that the earliest use of *christos* was in connection with Jesus' parousia rather than his resurrection or earthly ministry.[24] Certainly it is unique in Luke–Acts, for nowhere else is *christos* tied closely to the parousia and this alone is reason to suppose it is traditional material. Acts 2.36, on the other hand, appears to associate the designation *christos* with the resurrection–ascension, which does not accord with the announcement of messiahship at Jesus' birth (Luke 2.11, 26) or with the frequent references to the suffering of the Messiah (e.g., Luke 24.26, 46). Perhaps it too is traditional material, and to this we shall return below.

Our survey of Luke's use of *kurios* and *christos* has dealt with Luke's two major christological terms. The other titles are not insignificant but are, in one way or another, normally subsumed under these two. Most, if not all, of them are traditional and indicate that Luke's 'tendency is to use the normal terminology of the Church'.[25] The one possible exception is the title 'Saviour' (*soter*). In Luke 1.47 it is used of God and in Luke 2.11; Acts 5.31; 13.23 of Jesus. In Acts 5.31 it is connected closely with *archegos* (cf. Acts 7.35), a term used elsewhere only in Acts 3.15. In view of the importance of the cognate terms *soteria/soterion* (cf. Luke 1.6, 9, 71, 77; 2.30; 3.6; 19.9; Acts 4.12; 7.25; 13.26, 47; 16.17; 27.34; 28.28) and *sozo* (thirty times in Luke–Acts), the title *soter* is probably more significant than its few occurrences might suggest.[26]

The immediate contexts of Luke 2.11 and Acts 13.23 recall the Old Testament and Jewish use of the term. Luke 2.11 clearly associates *soter* with *christos* and *kurios* and alludes back to the Benedictus (cf. Luke 1.69 f), while in Acts 13.23 it says, 'Of this man's posterity God has brought to Israel a Saviour, Jesus, as he promised'. Both verses implicitly date the designation 'Saviour' from his birth. In Acts 5.31 *soter* is connected closely to *archegos* and associated with Jesus' exaltation: 'God exalted him at his right hand as Leader and Saviour' (cf. Heb. 2.10; 12.2; 2 Clem. 20.5). The other use of *archegos* in Luke–Acts (*archegos tes zoes* Acts 3.15), while obscure, probably refers to Jesus as the first one resurrected and the one who therefore guarantees resurrection and life to his own (cf. Acts 26.23).[27] There is thus a loose connection with Acts 5.31 (resurrection–exaltation), but the latter still stands somewhat out on a limb, recalling the Greek rather than the Jewish parallels to *soter* and *archegos*. And of course even in Luke 2.11; Acts 13.23 the Hellenistic and cosmic connotations of *soter* would not have been lost on Luke or his readers (cf. Heb. 2.10).

The remaining christological categories can be treated more briefly. Jesus' descent from David, a frequent theme in early Christianity (cf. Mark 10.47 pars.; 12.35 pars.; John 7.41; Rom. 1.3; Rev. 5.5; 22.16; Ign. *Eph.* 18.12; 20.2, etc.), comes to expression in Luke 1.26–38; 2.1–20, and Acts 13.22 f. On the whole it is a claim that is assumed rather than emphasized, as a comparison with Matthew shows (Matt. 1.1, 20; 9.27; 12.23; 15.22, etc.).

'Son of God' is taken over from Mark in Luke 3.22; 4.3, 9, 41; 8.28; 9.35; 10.22; 22.70, but otherwise occurs only in the birth narratives (Luke 1.32, 35) and the preaching attributed to Paul

(Acts 9.30; 13.33). For Luke it is apparently an equivalent of 'Messiah' (Luke 4.4; 22.70; Acts 9.20, 22; 13.33). Precisely when he thought Jesus became son he does not say. Assuming that *egeiren* in Acts 13.33 refers to the resurrection (cf. v. 34, and contrast Acts 3.22; 7.37), the quotation of Ps. 2.7 here suggests that Jesus became son at his resurrection. Yet in Luke 3.23, if we follow the Western reading, Ps. 2.7 is used to imply that his sonship is to be dated at the latest from his baptism (cf. Luke 9.35). To add to the confusion, Luke 1.32, 35 appear to imply that his sonship is to be dated from his birth, unless in both instances the future *klethesetai* is to be taken as a reference either to his baptism (cf. Acts 10.38)[28] or to his resurrection. In view of Luke 1.32 f and 3.22 it is most likely that in Acts 13.33 Luke uses an earlier adoptionist tradition without adjusting it to statements made elsewhere.[29] Indeed, together with the allusion to Davidic sonship in v. 22 f, Acts 13 can be seen as an expression of the so-called two-stage christology which is usually presumed to lie behind Rom. 1.3–4.[30]

In Luke, Jesus is frequently proclaimed as a prophetic figure by his audience (Luke 7.16, 39; 9.8; 24.19)—a view he apparently did not discourage (Luke 4.24; 13.33). The more specific role of Mosaic eschatological prophet (Deut. 18.15–18), which may well have been an important category in the early Christian understanding of Jesus,[31] is unambiguously ascribed to Jesus in Acts 3.22 f. However, even if a further allusion is found in Acts 7.35 f, and it is tenuous at best, it cannot be called a major theme. It is a traditional category which Luke finds useful, and which accords with his stress on Jesus as the fulfilment of the Old Testament and as a miracle worker (Acts 2.22; 10.38).

As it is used in Acts 4.27, 30, *pais* is a Davidic, messianic designation (cf. *Did.* 9.2 f; 10.2 f; 1 Clem. 59.2 f; *Mart. Polyc.* 14.1, 3; 20.2, etc.)[32] and the same meaning is probably to be assumed in Acts 3.13, 26, though an allusion to the Servant figure of Isaiah,[33] or the Mosaic prophet[34] cannot be excluded. The designations *hagios* (Acts 3.14, cf. 4.27, 30) and *dikaios* (Acts 3.14; 7.52; 22.14) may retain a certain moral tinge (cf. Luke 23.47),[35] but fit in well with Luke's other Messianic and prophetic categories. If they, like *pais*, do recall the Servant of Isaiah[36] then it is to express the innocent suffering of Jesus and not the expiatory significance of his death.

Most, if not all, of the christological titles we have surveyed were, from Luke's standpoint, traditional. This does not necessarily mean that they were all early terms; it simply indicates that none of them were coined by Luke. Some would have been familiar to him from everyday usage (e.g., *kurios*), others may have come down in liturgical form (e.g., *pais*), and yet others in summaries of Christian belief. It may be that he sometimes had good reason to believe that a certain usage (e.g., the titular *christos*) reflected ancient practice. Or perhaps any historical accuracies are fortuitous, the result of a haphazard use of traditional terminology which, by the law of averages, inevitably is sometimes correct.

It is clear that the narratives, kerygmatic summaries, and christological titles concur in their presentation of Lucan christology as an 'exaltation christology'. This central Lucan emphasis has some important corollaries. By adding the ascension to the narrative which he has already begun with an account of a supernatural birth Luke, more than any other Gospel writer, suggests parallels between Jesus and the Hellenistic 'divine men' and 'immortals'.[37] This was one way, among others, in which the significance of Jesus could be expressed.

A second consequence of Luke's concentration on the exaltation is that there is no emphatic *theologia crucis*. The death of Jesus is part of the kerygma, but viewed on the one hand as the fulfilment of the divine plan and on the other as the responsibility of the Jews. It is not an event which, in its own right, substantially affects the course of redemption. It is but one step on the road to glory. Third, the emphasis on the exaltation of Jesus appears to have diminished the importance of the parousia. It is mentioned (Acts 1.11; 3.20; 17.31) but is not a significant theme. Luke, like the early Church before him, has allowed the centre of gravity to shift from parousia to exaltation. The relationship between this exalted Lord and the believer is not conveyed in the same intimate terms as in Paul, but it is inadequate to characterize him as an absent or inactive Lord. For while such a notion may be found in Acts 3.20–1, these verses are in this respect, as in many others, atypical.[38]

Lucan christology, as Conzelmann has shown,[39] clearly subordinates Jesus to God—a traditional emphasis, but one which Luke readily adopts. This is perhaps clearest in the statements concerning Jesus' resurrection and exaltation (Acts 2.32–3; 3.15;

4.10; 5.30–1), but it is also God who declares that Jesus is his son (Luke 3.22; 9.35) and who works miracles through him (Acts 2.22). God appoints Jesus as Christ and Lord (Acts 2.36) and other titles express the same subordination. Certainly *kurios* and *soter* can be used of God and Jesus, but at this stage no advanced christological conclusions are drawn from this. The references to Jesus as a man confirm this (*aner* Acts 2.22; 17.31).

Undoubtedly this is the burden of Luke's message but, as Conzelmann is quick to point out, it does not stand alone. Jesus can act autonomously (Acts 10.38), for example, or the bestowal of the Spirit can be ascribed to him (Acts 2.33, cf. 5.32). With respect to God Jesus is subordinate, but with respect to the world he is pre-eminent and, on an experiential level, often indistinguishable from the Father. That is why both God and Jesus can be called Lord and Saviour and why the gift of the Spirit is seen to have its source in both. In other circles this leads to refinement or abolition of the notion of subordination, but for Luke apparently not. Indeed he shows little or no sign of reflection on these matters and, despite the use of the birth traditions (Luke 1—2), there is no assertion of Jesus' pre-existence in his work. It is unlikely that he would have been averse to such a notion, but it is significant that he does not consider it sufficiently important to mention.

C. H. Talbert detects an anti-gnostic motif in Luke's christology.[40] On the one hand, the materiality of the resurrection and ascension is emphasized in the distinctive references to 'body' in Luke 23.55; 24.3, 22–3, the special Lucan appearance described in Luke 24.36–43, and in the stress on the visibility of the ascension in Acts 1.9–11. On the other hand, the continuity between the earthly and exalted Jesus is stressed by the foreshadowing of the ascension in the Gospel and the presence of a constant group of eyewitnesses. The aim is to refute those who deny the reality of the death and resurrection and the physicality of the ascension. Luke confirms the real humanity of Jesus and denies the separation of his spirit and flesh. Talbert finds a similar theme in the account of Jesus' baptism, where the spirit descending 'in bodily form' discourages a separation of the spirit and flesh of Jesus, and in the birth narratives where the announcement of his divine sonship (Luke 1.31–5) forestalls the supposition that his divine nature first joined him at his baptism. Talbert's argument is stronger on the resurrection than on the baptism or ascension, but in neither case

is it overwhelming. The evidence he cites for gnostic reinterpreta-
tion of Jesus' resurrection and ascension (Iren., *Adv. Haer.*
1.30.12–14; 1.24.3–6; 1.26.1) is mainly concerned with a reinter-
pretation of Jesus' death. If the resurrection and ascension are
recast, it is only as a consequence of a new perspective on his death.
Talbert's supposition that, 'since no one defends what is secure',
there must be opponents in mind is also problematic, for not every
positive assertion has to be seen as a reaction to its opposite. In
this case, for example, it might simply be that Luke has a concrete
cast of mind, one which views things in tangible, material terms.
He may be emphasizing the corporeality of these events because
that is the way he understood them, and not because he is countering claims to the contrary. Finally, if a note of antagonism is to be
found, it is better to label it anti-docetic, since docetism and
gnosticism do not always coincide.

The abiding impression left by our survey of the Lucan writings
is that Luke has used diverse, and often ancient, christological
traditions without integrating them into any particular scheme.
This leads to a certain lack of uniformity, a disjunction between
different strands of material which stand side by side. Thus there
is a tension between the sequence of events in Acts 1 and the statements in Luke 24.1 f; Acts 2.32–3; 5.30–1. The use of christological titles is somewhat haphazard. They represent the terminology of Luke's day but, in many cases, the belief of the early
Church as well. Some may have had an archaic ring and were for
that reason deemed appropriate to the sermons of the early
Church.

Other examples are not difficult to find. Acts 3.19–21 almost
certainly contains pre-Lucan tradition,[41] possibly originating in
Baptist circles,[42] which is lodged uneasily in the Lucan context.
The emphasis on the parousia, or repentance that hastens the end,
and on *apokatastasis*, as well as the rather clumsy attempt to
subsume them under the scheme of prophecy and fulfilment,
suggests that this is so.[43] Acts 13 probably represents a two-stage
christology which cannot easily be reconciled with other statements about Jesus' divine sonship in Luke–Acts.[44] Some think
Acts 2.36 is a pre-Lucan, adoptionist confession of a similar kind,[45]
but the arguments are not persuasive. It is probably a Lucan
statement, subordinationist but not adoptionist in form, designed
to summarize the speech and contrast the actions of God and men

with respect to Jesus[46] or, less probably, to effect a compromise between conflicting christologies.[47] But the ambiguity is in itself significant, for it is indicative of the looseness, even carelessness, of Luke's christological language. It can be read in an adoptionist fashion even though that may not have been Luke's intention.

Thus while certain Lucan preferences, such as exaltation christology, are made clear, he also uses a great variety of christological material without obvious signs of reflection. One could put this down to his catholic taste, or perhaps to a tension between the expression of his own view and the attempt to report the views of others several decades earlier. But this is not the whole story. Luke, it appears, was a somewhat indiscriminating collector of christological traditions who transmits a variety of traditional terms and concepts without reflecting upon them individually or in conjunction with each other.

A survey of the christology of the Pastorals can be briefer, for there is less material, more agreement among commentators, and there are few historical problems. The seminal work by H. Windisch has, with good reason, gained the assent of most subsequent writers, and I shall be no exception.[48]

Kurios is used seventeen times in the Pastorals, mostly of Jesus (1 Tim. 1.2, 12; 6.3, 14; 2 Tim. 1.8, 16, 18; 2.7; 3.11; 4.8, 14, 22) but sometimes of God (1 Tim. 1.14; 2 Tim. 1.18; 2.19, 24), and in some instances could refer to either. Sometimes the fuller formulae 'Jesus Christ our Lord' (1 Tim. 1.2, 12) or 'our Lord Jesus Christ' (1 Tim. 6.3, 14) are used, but otherwise it is simply 'our Lord' or 'the Lord'. While the term retains a titular sense, especially in the fuller formulae, the overall impression is that it has become the normal way of referring to Jesus, the conventional form of Christian address which springs most naturally to mind. It can be used in formulae of greeting (1 Tim. 1.2) or blessing (2 Tim. 1.16, 18; 2.7; 4.22) and here, as elsewhere, it refers to the living, exalted Lord and his present functions (1 Tim. 1.12; 2 Tim. 1.8; 3.11), who strengthens his own in times of trial and persecution, to whom they testify before men (2 Tim. 1.8), and on whose 'sound words' they base their faith (1 Tim. 6.3). Jesus as *kurios* is also associated with the last things, especially judgement (1 Tim. 6.14; 2 Tim. 1.18; 4.8, 14), but this is not a special association of the title as such. It is used here because it is the appropriate way of addressing Jesus in any context, whether in his historical (1 Tim. 6.3), exalted (1 Tim. 1.12; 2 Tim. 3.11; 4.22, etc.) or future (1 Tim. 6.14, etc.) roles.

Saviour (*soter*) is used four times of Christ (2 Tim. 1.10; Tit. 1.4; 2.13; 3.6) and six times of God (1 Tim. 1.1; 2.3; 4.10; Tit. 1.3; 2.10; 3.4), showing the same easy oscillation as *kurios* (especially Tit. 1.3–4; 2.10, 13; 3.4–6).[49] In Tit. 1.4 'Saviour' is part of the epistolary greeting, but his activity is implicitly understood to be present. The life and immortality brought through his incarnation (2 Tim. 1.10) and his gift of the Spirit at baptism (Tit. 3.6) imply the same, while in Tit. 2.13 it is used in connection with his future coming. Several occurrences emphasize the universality of salvation (1 Tim. 2.3 f; 4.10; Tit. 2.10 f) in connection with God, and presumably the same applies to Jesus too. Whether it is consciously asserted in opposition to gnostic exclusivism is less certain. Saviour, in the Pastorals, whether used of God or Jesus, recalls Hellenistic rather than Old Testament language as the associations in 2 Tim. 1.10 (*photisantos de zoen kai aphtharsian*) and Tit. 3.4 (*chrestotes, philanthropia*) indicate. But a distinctively Christian element is not absent either, as Tit. 3.4 f shows.

Christos in the Pastorals is a proper name. The titular sense, even in the more solemn formulae, is lost. The extent of this shift is indicated by its use in 1 Tim. 2.6 of Jesus the 'man' and in 1 Tim. 6.13 of Jesus at his trial, neither of which so much as hints at the original connotations of the term. The Pauline phrase 'in Christ' occurs several times in the Pastorals (1 Tim. 1.14; 3.13; 2 Tim. 1.1, 9, 14; 2.1, 10; 3.12, 15) but in a stereotyped and non-Pauline manner.[50] In seven of the nine occurrences it is associated with an abstract noun (faith, love, grace, etc.) and has become a 'which is in Christ' formula uncharacteristic of Paul. Indeed the hymn or creed quoted in 2 Tim. 2.11–13, which does not use *en christo*, is in substance closer to the Pauline *en christo* than the uses of this phrase in the Pastorals!

1 Tim. 2.5–6 provides the only other example of a christological title in the Pastorals:

> For there is one God, and there is one mediator (*mesites*) between God and men, the man Christ Jesus, who gave himself as a ransom for all, the testimony to which was borne at the proper time.

The term *mesites* is used with a variety of connotations—legal, soteriological, and cosmological (cf. Philo, *Vit. Mos.* 2.16; *Rer. div. her.* 206; Plutarch, *Isis* 46.269E),[51] and the precise meaning here must be determined by the context. It is startling to find the mediator defined so unequivocally as a man, for the logic of the preceding statement would appear to require the mediator to be a God-man, a kind of hybrid representing the two divided parties. Yet this is not so. It is as a man that Jesus is called *mesites*. The emphasis on a single human mediator may be in contrast to the host of angelic intermediaries in some gnostic systems,[52] and there may be an anti-docetic strain too. But the blunt assertion of Jesus' humanity remains, even if he is in some sense a special man, like Moses in Jewish tradition (Gal. 3.19). Certainly he is the sole mediator, but that this claims uniqueness and not divine status the emphasis on 'one God' makes clear. The only other christological uses of *mesites* in the New Testament associate it with mediation of the covenant (Heb. 8.6; 9.15; 12.24) and this may be hinted at in 1 Tim. 2.6, where he is described as giving himself as a 'ransom for all' (cf. Mark 10.45). There is no suggestion that the mediator was pre-existent or that the payment of ransom followed a descent from the divine world (contrast Phil. 2.6–11). The title describes the vicarious self-offering of a man and not the *kenosis* of a god.

Clearly, *kurios* and *soter* are the most significant titles in the Pastorals. But, as with Luke, the titles are not the most important expression of christology. To find this we must turn to the miscellany of sayings, creeds, and confessions quoted at random throughout the letters. In these the author brings to expression his christological preferences, though, in view of his penchant for quoting remarkably diverse material, it is doubtful whether we can speak of *a* christology of the Pastorals at all.[53]

We can do no better than provide a brief synopsis of the relevant passages along the lines suggested by Windisch who, while occasionally overstating his case by a readiness to blend various statements into one point of view, in all important respects provides the definitive statement. One relevant passage, 1 Tim. 2.5–6, we have already discussed, where the emphasis is on the humanity of Jesus and nothing is said about his pre-existence. A not dissimilar statement is found in 2 Tim. 2.8.

Remember Jesus Christ, risen from the dead, descended from David, as preached in my gospel.

Two events in Jesus' career are isolated—his birth and his resurrection. It is probably an early confessional formula, expressing a two-stage christology such as is found in the pre-Pauline version of Rom. 1.3–5 (cf. Acts 13.22 f).[54] If one assumes that *en dunamei*, at least, is a Pauline addition, the remaining statement differs from 2 Tim. 2.8 in two ways: first, the contrast between the two stages is extended by their characterization as *kata sarka* and *kata pneuma* and second, the post-resurrection phase is associated with the title 'son of God'. Both of these, however, may be refinements of an earlier and simpler formula, close to that which has come down to us in 2 Tim. 2.8. It is important to note that pre-existence is not implied in this early formula, and most scholars think Paul added *en dunamei* to Rom. 1.3–4 precisely for this reason. Two-stage christology deals with the earthly and subsequent heavenly life of Jesus, without reference to a pre-existent stage.

In 1 Tim. 6.13–16 a similar tone is set:

> In the presence of God who gives life to all things, and of Christ Jesus who in his testimony before Pontius Pilate made the good confession, I charge you to keep the commandment unstained and free from reproach until the appearing of our Lord Jesus Christ; and this will be made manifest at the proper time by the blessed and only sovereign, the King of kings and Lord of lords, who alone has immortality and dwells in unapproachable light, whom no man has ever seen or can see. To him be honour and eternal dominion. Amen.

The exhortation to obedience (v. 14) is based on three factors: their past baptismal confession, the omnipresence of God and Jesus, and the future parousia. Embedded here is an implicit two-part christology which refers on the one hand to the earthly life of Jesus, particularly his trial (v. 13), and on the other hand to his future, heavenly parousia (v. 14). It is akin to the two-stage christology of 2 Tim. 2.8 in that there is no pre-existent stage, but differs in that the second stage is associated with the parousia rather than the resurrection. Both forms, however, are undoubtedly early. In this passage the references to God overshadow the christological allusions, for it is he who is creator (v. 13) who alone is the immortal Sovereign (cf. *monos* vv. 15–16). Windisch comments appropriately: 'Strictly speaking, beside the confession of the unique sovereignty of God there is room only for an "adoptionist christology".'[55] Perhaps 'subordinationist' rather than 'adoptionist' would be more accurate in this context, but in general the three passages we have considered do imply adoptionism insofar as they do not assert Jesus' pre-existence.

There is, however, at least one other strand in the Pastorals. In 1 Tim. 1.15, one of the faithful sayings, it is claimed that 'Christ Jesus came into the world (*elthen eis ton kosmon*) to save sinners'— a saying which, incidentally, is very close to Luke 19.10. The verb 'came' may imply pre-existence,[56] but is probably used in the general sense which means only that he was born into the world. In this case it says no more than 2 Tim. 2.8.

2 Tim. 1.9–10 is thought by many to contain an implicit reference to Jesus' pre-existence:[57]

> Who saved us and called us with a holy calling, not in virtue of our works but in virtue of his own purpose and the grace which he gave us in Christ Jesus ages ago (*pro chronon aionion*), and now has manifested through the appearing of our Saviour Jesus Christ (*tes epiphaneias tou Soteros hemon Christou Iesou*), who abolished death and brought life and immortality to light through the gospel.

'The epiphany of our Saviour' recalls the uses of *epiphaneia* elsewhere in the Pastorals—in an eschatological sense in 1 Tim. 6.14; 2 Tim. 4.1 (8); Tit. 2.13, and of the appearance of God's grace and goodness in Tit. 2.11; 3.4. Only in 2 Tim. 1.10 (and possibly 4.8) does it certainly refer to Jesus' first manifestation, which is seen to have been part of the divine plan 'before all eternity' (*pro chronon aionion*). The manifestation on earth alludes primarily, though not exclusively,[58] to the resurrection and the benefits which flow from it. The phrase 'grace which he gave us in Christ Jesus ages ago' is somewhat obscure (cf. Tit. 1.2–3), for while it is certain that it alludes to God's eternal plan of salvation it is not clear that it assumes the personal pre-existence of Jesus, through whom this salvation was subsequently mediated. If the latter is inferred, there is no doubt that the stress lies elsewhere. Brox justifiably claims that 'the explicit conception of a pre-existent Redeemer here remains blurred, if not wholly in the background'.[59]

The hymn or creed quoted in 1 Tim. 3.16 includes a reference to Jesus' first coming:

> He was manifested in the flesh,
> Vindicated in the Spirit,
> Seen by angels,
> Preached among the nations,
> Believed on in the world
> Taken up in glory.

The opening line (*hos ephanerothe en sarki*), in view of the use of *phaneroo* elsewhere (John 1.31; Heb. 9.36; 1 Pet. 1.20, etc.), may imply incarnation and pre-existence.[60] But if so, it is only implicit and is not referred to again. The burden of the hymn is undoubtedly the resurrection–exaltation and the events proceeding from it. The exaltation is certainly referred to in line 6 (cf. Luke 9.52; Acts 1.2, 11, 22) and probably in lines 2 and 3 as well, while lines 4 and 5 refer to post-exaltation events.[61] His entrance onto the scene (line 1) merely sets the stage for his exit (lines 2–6). There is no clear three-stage christology such as we find in the hymn in Phil. 2.6–11, and if it is implied one cannot fail to notice that the first two stages are compressed into one line. Moreover, not only the earthly life in general, but also the death of Jesus in particular, recedes with the emphasis on exaltation.

In summary, assertions of Jesus' pre-existence and divine nature in the Pastorals are, at the most, implicit. 1 Tim. 3.16 affords the best evidence, and one might add 2 Tim. 1.9 and 1 Tim. 1.15 in that order of likelihood. It is never an explicit theme in its own right, nor is it a major emphasis. One passage, however, might belie this conclusion, Tit. 2.13:

> awaiting our blessed hope, the appearing of the glory of our great God and (our) Saviour Jesus Christ (*epiphaneian tes doxes tou megalou Theou kai Soteros hemon Christou Iesou*).

Is Jesus identified with 'our great God'? The Greek is ambiguous and the arguments evenly balanced. In favour of an identification the following arguments have been used:[62] the presence of only one article; the Hellenistic parallels to 'God and Saviour' as a single designation; the natural association of the parousia with Jesus; and the use of *epiphaneia* elsewhere in the Pastorals only of the appearance of Christ (except possibly 2 Tim. 4.8). These are weighty arguments, though the absence of a second article is not inexplicable,[63] and the association of God with the parousia not entirely inappropriate. The scarcity of direct identifications of Christ and God elsewhere in the New Testament is not an overwhelming counter-argument, though the tendency of the Pastorals clearly to distinguish elsewhere God and Christ when they are mentioned together, and to emphasize both the humanity of Jesus and the uniqueness of God, does make one hesitate to identify them in Tit. 2.13. The problem with this argument, however, is that the Pastorals are such a patchwork of quotations and show so few signs of theological reflection that one can never be sure that it is legitimate to use one passage to interpret another.

The dilemma of Tit. 2.13 is the dilemma of the christology of the Pastorals as a whole and, indeed, what is true of the christology of the Pastorals is true of the Pastorals in general. Certain preferences can be detected. Creeds, hymns, and summaries of Christian belief are more important than titles, though the use of *kurios* and *soter* are significant. There is an apparent preference for 'exaltation' christology, expressed in the twofold structure of 2 Tim. 2.8; 1 Tim. 6.13 f and overwhelmingly in 1 Tim. 3.16, where both the earthly (cf. 1 Tim. 2.5) and the post-ascension periods have their role. Consistent with this, though not obviously integrated, is the emphasis on the uniqueness of God (1 Tim. 2.5; 6.15–16) and the consequent subordination of Jesus. On the other hand, there are passages which either imply Jesus' pre-existence (1 Tim. 3.16; 2 Tim. 1.9 f) or are at least sufficiently ambiguous to allow such an interpretation, and one passage which might identify Christ and God. Moreover there are several references to the parousia (1 Tim. 6.14; 2 Tim. 4.1, 8; Tit. 2.13), often with Jesus in the role as judge, which are not in any way integrated with the exaltation theme.

To decide from this hotchpotch of evidence what the view of the Pastor was, is no mean task. If one is to prefer that which he states clearly to that which he merely implies, then the exaltation–subordination strand would carry the day. One could go further, in view of the indisputable implications of 1 Tim. 2.5, and assert that the divinity of Jesus cannot be implied in Tit. 2.13 and that the apparent allusions to pre-existence are unintentional. We would then begin to get a consistent picture. But this would be to impose consistency where it probably does not belong. Throughout the letters the Pastor gives the impression of having a practical and unoriginal turn of mind, one which eschews speculation and innovation in favour of the faithful transmission of tradition. In this light, the presence of conflicting christologies would be understandable, for he simply passes on what he receives and what he receives comes from different eras and different places. Some of his statements concur with the christology of the man in whose name he writes, while others Paul would firmly have amended. Some snippets of tradition may reflect very early beliefs (e.g., 2 Tim. 2.8) while other terms (e.g., *soter*) may have originated at a later date. His use of this traditional material was uncritical and naive. He offers no synthesis, and little or no interpretation. His purpose appears to have been limited to the preservation and inculcation of that which he received. That this produced tensions, and occasionally even contradictions, appears not to have concerned him, or to have escaped his notice altogether.

There is something to the view that what unity there is in the christology of the Pastorals 'results from the constant emphasis upon the meaning of salvation for the present'. However, the references to the parousia should not be ignored, and the presence of several christological concepts side by side conveying 'a strangely undefined relationship between God and Christ',[64] is not made any the less strange by the emphasis on present salvation. Nor can one find unity in an anti-gnostic stance for, although a few statements might have an anti-docetic ring (1 Tim. 2.5–6; 3.16; 2 Tim. 2.8), since they insist on Jesus' real humanity and the reality of his death and resurrection, they do not set the overall tone.

How do the christologies of Luke–Acts and the Pastorals compare? There is a remarkable number of similarities. First, there is a congruity in their choice of christological titles, while in neither case are they the authors' major christological expression. For both, *kurios* is the common and natural form of address, associated particularly but not exclusively with the exalted, present Lord. *christos* is frequent in both, though the technical sense is absent in the Pastorals. But this is because of the difference in both genre and circumstances. The Pastorals do not attempt to recreate the missionary apologetics of the early Church, and the opponents who might have revived the debates over messiahship when Luke wrote Acts were a spent force when the Pastorals were written. The order 'Christ Jesus' is preferred in the Pastorals and this finds a lone parallel in Acts 24.24. However, it is one of only two uses of this simple form as a proper name (cf. Acts 9.34), the remainder being either technical or fixed formulaic uses.

'Saviour' is used in much the same way by both writers. Only Luke–Acts and the Pastorals in the New Testament use it of both God and Jesus and, apart from 2 Peter, are the only ones to use it with any frequency. It is thus for both writers a chosen term which reflects both the high status of Jesus and the universality of the redemption he brings. The remaining title in the Pastorals, 'mediator', is not found in Luke–Acts, but Jesus' unique role in salvation expressed in Acts 4.12 says much the same thing. The absence from the Pastorals of several titles which occur in Acts is insignificant, since most of them occur rarely and always in subordination to *kurios* and *christos*.

Second, it is clear that exaltation christology is important for both writers. This is unmistakeable in the narrative and kerygmatic formulations peculiar to Luke. The primary evidence in the Pastorals is 1 Tim. 3.16, which accords remarkably with both the theology and the narrative structure of Acts, expressing both the exaltation of Jesus and the universal mission that ensued. In accord with this is the emphasis on Jesus' subordination and the references to a two-stage christology which can be found in both writers. It is with good reason that Windisch finds the closest parallels to the christology of the Pastorals in the speeches of Acts. This pattern remains unbroken in Luke–Acts, whereas in the Pastorals there are possible allusions to Jesus' pre-existence. The contrast is lessened when it is recognized that the latter are both unemphatic and undeveloped. They are certainly not the burden of his christological message. A concomitant of exaltation christology in both writers is the lack of emphasis on a *theologia crucis*. The cross is not a climax itself but a prelude to Jesus' climactic exaltation. There is in addition a marked emphasis on the humanity of Jesus. 1 Tim. 2.6 (*anthropos*) is an emphatic statement which is very close to Acts 2.22; 17.31 (*aner*), and although the terms are not the same, the meaning is.

Finally, and in many ways most importantly, Luke–Acts and the Pastorals exhibit a similar cast of mind. They both make free use of traditional material—titles, hymns, creeds, and christological summaries—with little discrimination. From our vantage point each writer uses material which creates internal tensions, if not contradictions; yet they themselves seem to be either unaware or unconcerned. The contrast with Paul is dramatic. He too can borrow traditional formulations, but rarely repeats them unchanged. He refines and corrects them, bringing them into line with his own convictions and integrating them into a consistent whole. Paul's eclecticism is creative and innovative, not passive and doctrinaire. Here, as so often, a comparison with Paul shows that Luke and the Pastor are as like each other as they are unlike him.

To conclude: Luke and the Pastor agree not only in terms of the content of their christological teaching, but also in their technique of compilation. It would not be unnatural to conclude that they were one and the same man.

8

Law and Scripture

There are some difficulties in comparing the attitudes of Luke and the Pastor on the themes of law and Scripture. In particular there is the indisputable fact that, whereas in Luke–Acts they are themes of considerable importance, in the Pastorals they receive scant attention. Some explanation of this has to be offered if one is to defend the theory of common authorship, but before this is attempted it is necessary to consider what the Pastorals *do* say and compare it with Luke–Acts. Such a discussion may well shed light on the broader problem.

The obvious statement to start with occurs in 1 Tim. 1.6–10:

> Certain persons by swerving from these have wandered away into vain discussion, desiring to be teachers of the law (*nomodidaskaloi*), without understanding either what they are saying or the things about which they make assertions. Now we know that the law is good, if anyone uses it lawfully (*nomimos*), understanding this, that the law is not laid down for the just (*dikaio*) but for the lawless and disobedient (*anomois de kai anupotaktois*), for the ungodly and sinners, for the unholy and profane, for murderers of fathers and murderers of mothers, for manslayers, immoral persons, sodomites, kidnappers, liars, perjurers, and whatever else is contrary to sound doctrine.

It is important in understanding the statements evaluating the law and its function to see them in context. They are primarily a reaction to the misleading and ignorant assertions of those who claim to be 'teachers of the law' (*nomodidaskaloi*). The word occurs only here in the Pastorals and, interestingly enough, elsewhere in the New Testament only in Luke 5.17; Acts 5.34. There it refers to Jewish teachers who are experts in expounding the law, and does not appear to have pejorative undertones. It is probable, therefore, that in 1 Tim. 1.7 the reference is likewise to Jews who consider themselves to be authoritative experts in the interpretation of the Old Testament. This would imply, like other material in the Pastorals, that the opponents of the Pastor were Jewish gnostics. At any rate, the statement that the law is good is not a reaction to antinomians who claim that the law is evil; rather, it is directed at those who would agree that the law is good, but who use it for illegitimate purposes. It is not clear whether the 'teachers of the law' were Christian or non-Christian, and one's decision is related to an overall assessment of the Pastor's opponents. In view of 1 Tim. 1.6 f, the allusion to disputes over the law in Tit. 3.9 (*machas nomikas*—the latter word is one which occurs elsewhere only in Tit. 3.13; Luke 7.30; 10.35; 11.45–6, 52–3; 14.3; and Matt. 22.35), and the frequent allusions to the propaganda of the false teachers, one can conclude that their 'vain discussions' led both to fantastic speculation (Tit. 3.4, etc.) and to ascetical prescriptions (cf. 1 Tim. 4.2–3) based on the Old Testament.[1] In the immediate context (1 Tim. 1.4) the emphasis (as in Tit. 3.9) is undoubtedly on the former abuse, though if one follows C. K. Barrett[2] and interprets 1 Tim. 1.7 to include the application of the law to the wrong people, the latter also plays a role. The Pastor's opponents, therefore, were not the Judaizers with whom Paul had to contend, who insisted on a rigid application of the law to all believers; rather, they were Jewish gnostics who used the Scriptures as the basis for their speculation and asceticism.

The response of the Pastor is to insist on a quite different, pragmatic evaluation of the law. A Pauline catch-phrase is quoted —'the law is good'—but then interpreted in a non-Pauline manner. The law is to be used *nomimos* (cf. 2 Tim. 2.5), which means 'lawfully' 'in the right way', and so 'in accordance with its nature as Law'.[3] This is immediately defined in v. 9, where the purpose of the law is seen to be prescriptive and concerned primarily with piety and ethics (which, for the Pastor, are virtually indistinguishable). The law's function as a guide to morals and piety is directly opposed to the speculative use of the law. It follows that the righteous have no need of the law, not because they are in any Pauline sense justified by faith through grace but, in line with the predominantly ethical use of *dikaios* and cognates in the Pastorals, because they already keep the law as godly and upright citizens.[4] The argument seems to be a curious combination of a Pauline catch-phrase, and the Stoic view that the law is directed only at the lawless (cf. Rom. 13.1 f).[5] There is something of a confusion between Torah and natural law or, at the least, the use of a Stoic principle as a means of understanding the purpose of the Torah.

It has often been noted that this view of the law is not one that can readily be attributed to Paul. It is true that his discussion of the law is complicated and at times obscure, and that his most radical statements about the law are confined almost exclusively to Romans and Galatians. However, since the Pastorals purport to be Pauline and the subject of law is broached, it is legitimate to point out the contrast with Paul's discussion of the problem elsewhere. First, the confusion between Torah and natural law is one which Paul clearly avoids both in his discussion of the condition of Jews and Gentiles *coram Deo* in Rom. 1—3 and in his discussion of the State in Rom. 13.1 f. Second, the notion that the law is good is thoroughly Pauline, but the corollary that its goodness lies in its restraint of evildoers is not: 'In what a different world of thought this stands from the noble Pauline conception of the law as the revelation of God's will and character, liable to abuse precisely when it is used "lawfully".'[6] The pedagogical purpose of the law, as Paul understood it—where men understand the goodness of the law precisely when they have broken it, where the law is understood to lead not to God but to sin and only as a result of this to point to God's mercy—is entirely foreign to the Pastorals. It is true that Paul can use the law as the basis for ethical prescription in a Christian's life (Rom. 13.8 f, etc.), but not before both the tyranny of the law and the freedom brought by the new revelation of God's righteousness have been carefully expounded. Thus, while the Pastor agrees with Paul on the goodness of the law and does not recommend the law as a way of salvation, he seems totally unaware of the religious problem of the law as Paul understood it. This is particularly obvious, as we have seen, in those passages which come closest to expressing the Pauline view of salvation (2 Tim. 1.9; Tit. 3.5–7), where the concept 'works of the law' is absent. It seems that the Pastor knew a Pauline phrase, perhaps from oral tradition, but did not fully understand the way Paul would have used it. As one writer puts it: 'In his effort to repeat Paul's criticism of the law, the writer has laid himself open to his own stricture on the false teachers that "they do not understand the things on which they insist".'[7]

The teaching of Luke–Acts is more complex,[8] for the issue of the law and its authority plays a larger role, though, as we shall see, the discussion is differently motivated from that of the Pastorals. Luke–Acts offers no fundamental criticism of the law as it applies to Jews and Jewish Christians. Luke's terminology with respect to the law is often peculiar to him and bears a marked Hellenistic–Jewish stamp.[9] Moreover, it is closely associated with the figure of Moses: the law is 'the customs which Moses delivered to us' (Acts 6.14; 15.1; 21.21; 28.17), 'the law of Moses' (Acts 6.11, 13, 14; 21.21, 28; 25.8; 28.17), and the name Moses alone refers regularly to the law (Luke 5.14; 16.29, 31; 24.27; Acts 6.11; 15.1, 21; 21.21). In Luke's Gospel, the question about the greatest commandment becomes one about the means of attaining eternal life (Mark 12.28 f; Luke 10.25 f), and the saying on divorce which suggests a conflict within the law is missing (Mark 10.2 f), as is the pericope on ritual cleanliness (Mark 7.1 f)—though this last is part of Luke's 'great omission'. The disputes over Sabbath law are designed to show that Jesus is in reality acting in accordance with the spirit of the law (Luke 6.1–5, 6–11; 12.10–17; 14.1–6), for the law stands as eternally valid (Luke 16.16–17). Consonant with this is the description in Acts of the Church and its leaders. The Jerusalem Christians continue to worship in the Temple and live according to the law (Acts 1—5), it is denied that Stephen attacked the law (Acts 6.11–14), and Peter shows great concern over the legal problems of dealing with Cornelius and his household (Acts 10.26; 11.3 f). Above all, Paul is portrayed as a devout, law-abiding Jew. This is clear in Acts 16.1 f where he has Timothy circumcised to forestall Jewish objections, in Acts 21.20 f where he takes a vow to convince Jerusalem Christians that he does not oppose Jewish–Christian adherence to the law, and in his repeated denial of the charge that he attacked the law (Acts 22.3; 23.1–6; 24.14 f; 26.4–5, 22 f). Jervell, in particular, has argued forcefully that Paul's speeches in Acts 22—6 are intended as a personal apology for Paul, asserting his innocence not from political, but from religious, wrong-doing.[10]

The key to understanding Luke's view of the law, however, lies in two other areas: first the relationship of the law to Gentile Christianity; and, second, the *Sitz im Leben* of Acts. These two factors, above all, colour an assessment of his statements about the law. In principle, the Cornelius narrative (Acts 10—11) decides the issue of the Gentiles and the law. Against his better judgement, and in violation of the law, Peter is compelled by a heavenly vision, a voice, and the Spirit to preach the Gospel to Cornelius' household. He becomes convinced that 'in every nation any one who fears him and does what is right is acceptable to him' (Acts 10.35) and this is confirmed by the outpouring of the Spirit on the Gentiles (Acts 10.45 f). Precisely the same combination of divine initiative and outpouring of the Spirit silences the circumcision party in Jerusalem and turns their opposition into praise (Acts 11.17–18). It is true that the dispute starts with the question of table-fellowship (Acts 11.3) but this simply illustrates the broader problem of the Gentiles and the law. If one were to read Acts 10—11 in isolation from Acts 15, the natural assumption would be that God had settled the Gentile issue once and for all: there is no longer a distinction between clean and unclean, Jew and non-Jew; all those who are pious and moral are acceptable to him, regardless of their origin. In other words, the law has no relevance to the Gentiles and any attempt to impose it upon them would contravene God's will. In Acts 15, however, the topic is aired a second time. The Pharisaic element in the Jerusalem church claims that 'it is necessary to circumcise them (Gentiles) and to charge them to keep the law of Moses' (Acts 15.5), a view which Paul and Barnabas hotly dispute (Acts 15.2). When a judgement is handed down by the Jerusalem leaders, new arguments are introduced. The will of God, as revealed in the Cornelius incident, is recalled by Peter and James (Acts 15.7–9, 14). In addition, Peter introduces two further considerations, one pragmatic and the other theological. The pragmatic argument is that the law is a burden which the Jews, not to mention the Gentiles, have been unable to bear (Acts 15.10, 28), while on a theological level it is claimed that both Jews and Gentiles depend upon the grace of God for salvation and, by implication therefore, not upon fulfilment of the law (Acts 15.10). To these arguments James adds the observation that the salvation of the Gentiles is a fulfilment of prophecy (Acts 15.15–18).

The somewhat unexpected upshot of these deliberations is the promulgation of the apostolic decree, in which the maximum demands placed on Gentiles are that they 'abstain from the pollutions of idols and from unchastity and from what is strangled and from blood. For from early generations Moses has had in every city those who preach him, for he is read every sabbath in the synagogues' (Acts 15.20–1). The origin and significance of this decree, the obscure justification for it (v. 21), as well as the apparent contradiction with Acts 10—11, have given rise to considerable debate. A connection between the demands of the decree and the rules governing the behaviour of non-Israelites in Lev. 17—18 is indisputable. J. Jervell thinks Luke is arguing that not only the Jews but also the Gentiles keep the law. That part of the law which traditionally applied to Gentiles (Lev. 17—18) is summarized and confirmed as the necessary obligation for Gentile Christians. It is thus, he argues, anomalous to speak of a law-free Gentile mission, since the Gentiles do keep that part of the law which applies to them. This is part of Jervell's broader argument that Luke sees the Church as the true Israel, consisting of Christian Jews and those Gentile converts who are grafted onto the main stem of Israel. Luke is thus consistently conservative in his attitude towards the law, since he believes that the Church, the true Israel, preserves the law and its demands. Jewish Christians come under all the regulations of the Mosaic law and Gentiles under those parts which apply to them. Jervell's view presupposes a situation in Luke's day where the Jewish Christians formed 'a respected and influential element', and where Church and synagogue are separate entities at enmity with each other.[11]

J. C. O'Neill offers a similar explanation but with a different slant. He thinks that in the community for whom Luke wrote, the Jewish Christians were a minority who were pleading with the Gentile majority to be allowed to continue their observance of the law. Luke takes the view that their plea should be accepted and proposes a *modus vivendi*, where neither side imposes its view on the other. The Gentiles would keep the rules of Lev. 17—18, but nothing more; in return, they would protect the right of Jewish Christians to live according to the Mosaic law. Accordingly, he interprets Acts 15.21 to mean that since there were synagogues in every major town, where the law was read and upheld, it was important for Gentile Christians, who would be associated with Jews, to observe the minimum cultic requirements laid down for Gentiles.[12] However O'Neill does not see this as the major purpose of Acts, for he thinks it was written primarily with an evangelistic purpose, to convince educated Roman readers of the truth of the gospel.

A third line of interpretation is to see the apostolic decree as a creation of Luke in which he expresses the common practice of his day. The Cornelius incident and the additional arguments put forward by Peter and James in Acts 15 are seen to be a formal recognition of the freedom of the Gentiles from the law:

> The modest conditions attached to this decision, enumerating certain requirements still regarded as 'necessary', are not seen by Luke as a limitation of this freedom; for by this time they had long been a universally recognised moral code for Christians, the validity of which was therefore in his eyes something taken for granted and which no one could find oppressive.[13]

Acts 15.21 would seem to indicate that Luke was aware of the connection between the demands of the decree and Lev. 17—18. Yet it is interesting to observe that in some ways he obscures this connection: Acts 15.21 is, in the oft-quoted words of Dibelius, 'so far as context and meaning are concerned, among the most difficult in the New Testament';[14] also, Acts 15.21 refers only to the 'necessity' of keeping these commandments and Acts 21.25 to the 'judgement' of the Apostles. If Luke's intention had been to show that the Gentiles do in fact keep the law, as Jervell supposes, he had ample opportunity to make this clear.

This lends support to von Campenhausen's view that Luke did not see the decree as in any sense imposing the law on the Gentiles. Perhaps then the emphasis in Acts 15.21 is on the phrase 'from early generations'; i.e., it had been a long-established practice in the diaspora for god-fearers or Gentiles who mixed socially with Jews to avoid certain practices offensive to them. The connection with Lev. 17—18 would often have been overlooked as it became a normal social practice—a practice continued by Gentile Christians. The advantage of this interpretation of Luke's view of the apostolic decree is that it fits more smoothly with Acts 10—11; 15.1–20, all of which seem to be leading up to a decision that the Gentiles should be freed from the law. It should be added that the notion that Luke composed the decree is not essential to this interpretation, for he may have received it as a piece of ecclesiastical tradition which coincidentally expressed what was already the practice in his community. Moreover, adherence to some of the rules, by the time Luke wrote, may have acquired additional motivations beyond the regulation of Jewish–Gentile relations. The prohibition of food offered to idols may have been related to the struggle with gnostics, and the marriage laws may simply reflect the laws of the State.[15]

The overall message that Luke intends, therefore—that Jewish Christians can continue to obey the law, but Gentiles are free from its demands—is in accord with Paul's view. Equally in accord with Paul is the view that the law is good, but does not offer a way of salvation (Acts 15.10; 13.39). But there are other ways in which Luke's statements about the law bear no relation to Paul's. The argument that the Gentiles should not be required to keep the law because it is burdensome (Acts 15.10, 28) is not the Pauline way of reasoning. The same can be said of Acts 13.38–9 which, although it echoes Paul's teaching, expresses in vague generalities what in Paul is far more complex and profound. As Haenchen succinctly expresses it: 'That the law occasions only wrath, and awakens not obedience but rather disobedience—such and similar statements Luke would have relegated to what 2 Pet. 3.16 calls *dusnoeta*, things difficult to understand, "which the ignorant and unstable distort".'[16]

Before we compare what Luke and the Pastor say on the law, it will be useful to consider their treatment of the Old Testament as Scripture. The crucial passage in the Pastorals is in 2 Tim. 3.15–17:

> from childhood you have been acquainted with the sacred writings (*hiera grammata*) which are able to instruct you for salvation through faith in Jesus Christ. All scripture is inspired by God (*pasa graphe theopneustos*) and profitable for teaching, for reproof, for correction, and for training in righteousness, that the man of God may be complete, equipped for every good work.

The phrase *hiera grammata* refers primarily to the Old Testament, as in Hellenistic Judaism (e.g., Philo, *Vit. Mos.* II. 202; Jos., *Ant.*, X. 210), though possibly some Christian writings are included too, a gospel or maybe some of Paul's writings (cf. 1 Tim. 5.13). *Pasa graphe theopneustos* is ambiguous and the RSV version above is probably not the most accurate; a better rendering would be, 'every inspired writing has its use'.[17] Again the reference is primarily to the Old Testament and, whether *pasa* refers to the Old Testament as a whole or to individual parts of it, the point is that the divinely inspired Scripture is good for teaching, reproof etc. Maybe, too, *graphe* includes any inspired religious writing, since in Tit. 1.12 the author quotes a pagan 'prophet' to good effect. In turn, this would recall Acts 17.28 where Luke uses quotations from a pagan poet to express the relationship between God and man (and is it wholly fortuitous that both Tit. 1.12 and Acts 17.28 may be quoting Epimenides?).[18]

Several comments are in order here: it is improbable that the assertions of 2 Tim. 3.15–16 are directed against opponents who question the inspiration of parts of the Old Testament.[19] Unlike the author of 2 Pet. 1.19–21, the Pastor is not interested in the fact or the nature of the inspiration of the Old Testament, but in the use to which these scriptures are put. He seems more concerned to oppose a speculative use of Scripture, which uses it as the basis for constructing a complex mythological system. He approves of the assertion that the Old Testament can instruct men in salvation through faith in Jesus Christ, but immediately forestalls any misunderstanding by making it clear what the purpose of these scriptures is. They are not designed to form the basis of an abstruse metaphysic or a complex mythology, but to instruct men in the proper lifestyle. Their purpose is down-to-earth and pragmatic—to teach, reprove, correct, and train believers so that they may be 'equipped for every good work'. They are, as it were, a source-book of ethical exhortation—in agreement with the purpose of the law as expressed in 1 Tim. 1.7 f. Doubtless the same thing is in mind when Timothy is exhorted to 'attend to the public reading of scripture, to preaching, to teaching' (1 Tim. 4.13).

The only specific quotation from the Old Testament in the Pastorals occurs in 1 Tim. 5.18:

> For the scripture (*graphe*) says: 'You shall not muzzle an ox when it is treading out the grain', and, 'The labourer deserves his wages (*tou misthou autou*)'.

This verse is relevant to our discussion in several ways. First, it apparently uses the Old Testament to support the author's judgement on the practical problem of the payment of church leaders, and is thus precisely the use of Scripture recommended in 2 Tim. 3.16. Second, it is just possible that the phrase is quoted from 1 Cor. 9.9 rather than from Deut. 25.4. Third, the claim that the 'labourer deserves his wages' recalls the identical Greek phrase in Luke 10.7 (Matt. 10.10 has *tes trophes autou* for Luke's *tou misthou autou*).[20] The connection with the peculiarly Lucan form of the saying is striking, especially since the phrase is not found in the Old Testament or in Jewish apocryphal writings. Maybe, therefore, the Pastor includes at least one Christian writing, Luke's Gospel, in *graphe*. This is not certain, however, since the saying may have appeared in Jewish writings no longer extant, and *graphe* may refer only to the first quotation (and therefore probably to Deut. 25.4), to which the proverb about the labourer is only loosely attached.

There is undeniably a certain tension between 2 Tim. 3.15–17 and 1 Tim. 1.6–10. They agree in their assessment of the primary function of the Old Testament—to serve as a guide for moral behaviour—but the one suggests that Christians have no need of it and the other that it is a very useful textbook for the instruction of believers. The contradiction might be lessened somewhat if *nomos* in 1 Tim. 1.8 is interpreted to mean exclusively the Pentateuch and in particular its legal portions. But even so *hiera grammata* and *pasa graphe* clearly include the Pentateuch. Perhaps we have too readily assumed that the statement in 1 Tim. 1.6–10 implies that Christians have no need of the law. Maybe the author is simply making a theoretical statement about the nature of the law: it is given to control lawlessness and acts as a form of compulsion, but if one is living by it, it no longer needs to compel. But he is perhaps not implying that in reality there are any such who do fully abide by the law or who are fully righteous. Indeed, the constant exhortations, including the one to pursue righteousness, imply the opposite. The ambiguity may have resulted from his rather muddled use of a Stoic proposition about law in general with reference to the Torah, and from his eagerness to cast moral aspersions on his opponents. We could then presume that at least one of the 'lawful' uses of the law is precisely that recommended in 2 Tim. 3.15–17. However we resolve the tension between these two passages, the conclusion remains that for the Pastor the main purpose of the scriptures was to provide a moral guideline, a basis for exhortation to, and the direction of, an upright Christian life.

Luke[21] uses direct quotations from the Old Testament approximately thirty five times, as well as frequent allusions to it (especially in Luke 1—2; Acts 7.1 f; 13.17 f). Of these, eight are from the Pentateuch (Luke 4.1–12; 18.20; Acts 3.21–3, 25; 23.5), two from

1 Samuel (Luke 1.46–55; 6.3–4), fourteen from the prophets, of which nine are from Isaiah (Luke 3.4–6; 4.18–19; 22.37; Acts 2.17–21; 7.42–3, 49–50; 8.32–3; 13.34, 41, 47; 15.16–18; 28.26–8) and eleven from the Psalms (Luke 20.17, 42; Acts 1.20; 2.25–8, 34–5; 4.11, 25; 13.33, 35; 28.28). The majority of these fall into the promise-fulfilment pattern (though cf. Luke 6.3–4; 18.20; Acts 7.1 f, 52; 13.34; 23.5). Luke adds little to his sources in the Gospel: apart from Luke 1—2, which recreates an aura of Old Testament piety and expectation, there is only the quotation of Isa. 61.1–2 in Luke 4.18–19—which is probably dependent to some degree on Luke 7.22 pars.—and the reference to Isa. 53.12 in Luke 22.37. In the description of Jesus' public ministry Luke rarely varies his sources, unlike Matthew who introduces a catena of proof–texts introduced by a quotation formula. The most important additions by Luke are in the post-resurrection period where, in Luke 24.26–7, 44–7, he clearly states his understanding of the relationship between Old Testament promise and its fulfilment in Jesus and where, by putting these words on the lips of Jesus, he authorizes the scriptural exegesis and teaching of the Church. For it is not only to the Old Testament that Jesus points but also to his own teaching (Luke 24.44), which includes his own authoritative interpretation of these scriptures. Perhaps it is because this is located in the post-resurrection period that the utilization of 'proof from prophecy', though exemplified by Jesus and programmatically authorized by him, is primarily an activity of the church era.

Luke 24.44–7 is the most comprehensive statement in Luke–Acts about the nature of the Old Testament as promise and its fulfilment in Christ:

> Then he said to them, 'These are my words which I spoke to you, while I was still with you, that everything written about me in the law of Moses and the prophets and the psalms must be fulfilled.' Then he opened their minds to understand the scriptures, and said to them, 'Thus it is written, that the Christ should suffer and on the third day rise from the dead, and that repentance and forgiveness of sins should be preached in his name to all nations, beginning from Jerusalem.'

Here, in a nutshell, we have Luke's view of Scripture. That it is divinely inspired is assumed. It is a revelation of the will of God, expressing his predestined purpose for the world. The Scriptures, even the law, are primarily prophetic, their purpose being to foretell the salvation that is now present and the suffering Messiah who brings it. And when one reviews those passages where Luke uses the Old Testaments a promise—apart from a few which relate specifically to the defection of Judas (Acts 1.20), Pentecost (Acts 2.17–21), the Temple and its cult (Luke 19.46, cf. Acts 7.42–3, 49–50)—they are seen to cover three main themes: the Messianic era in general (Luke 1.46 f; 4.18–19; Acts 3.24); the coming of Christ, his death, resurrection, and exaltation (Luke 22.37; Acts 2.25–8, 34–5; 8.22–3; 13.34–5); and the rejection of Jesus by the Jews and his acceptance by the Gentiles (Luke 20.17; Acts 3.25; 4.25; 13.41, 47; 15.16–18; 28.26–8). In addition there are several general statements which, while they contain no direct quotations, speak of the promise-fulfilment theme (Luke 24.26–7; Acts 3.18; 10.43; 13.22–9, 32–3; 17.2–3; 18.28; 26.22–3). These general statements are spread throughout Acts, though direct quotations are, apart from 28.26–8, curiously absent from Acts 16—28. To complete the picture, it should be noted that references to prophecy and fulfilment are restricted to those occasions where the Church is preaching to or disputing with Jews. When faced with a Gentile audience a quite different line of argument is pursued, to the point where quotations from pagan poets are substituted for Old Testament prophecy (Acts 14.15–17; 17.22–31, esp. v. 28).

Within Luke's indisputable conviction that every important turn of events is part of God's promised and predetermined plan, two themes stand out, not only in the programmatic statement of Luke 24.44–7, but also in the actual employment of quotations: the death and resurrection of Jesus, and the Gentile mission. There is little doubt that Luke accurately reflects two of the central disputes in the early Church as it attempted to come to terms with its Jewish heritage. Clearly, for several decades no single solution to either problem was adopted by all Christians; but whatever theological conclusions or practical arrangements were made, they were motivated to a large degree by a belief that Jesus was the promised Messiah and by the necessity of accommodating a rapidly increasing number of Gentile converts. As we shall see below, however, there was probably more than a mere antiquarian interest in Luke's description of the early Church. An apologetic note, related to the situation of the Church in his day, is not difficult to detect. But before we discuss this we can summarize our conclusions on law and Scripture.

Both Luke–Acts and the Pastorals agree that the law is good, and is a genuine revelation of God's will, but that it is inadequate as a way of salvation. They also agree that salvation depends on the grace of God as revealed in Jesus Christ. And when they express this conviction, purporting to give the opinion of Paul by attribution of a speech or letter to him, it is in language which is reminiscent of Paul but which fails to convey either the complexity or the profundity of his view of the law. They both lack the precision and bite which Paul brings to the issues, preferring watered-down generalities. In each case one is left with the impression of a writer who relies on loose expressions of Pauline teaching, perhaps received only in oral form, and who stands at a considerable distance from the controversies which originally animated their author. With regard to Scripture they have one common conviction, explicit in both cases, namely that the Old Testament is divinely inspired and profitable for Christians' use (Acts 4.25; 2 Tim. 3.16). In addition, they are both prepared to quote from pagan 'prophets' when it suits their purpose.

There are, however, some striking differences which it is now our task to consider. For Luke the problem of the law is both an internal and an external issue for the Church. Externally, the Church faced Jewish accusations that it attacked the law, and these Luke bluntly denies. Internally, the problem was twofold. On the one hand, there were Jewish Christians in Jerusalem who accused Paul of encouraging other Jewish Christians (in the diaspora) to abandon the law—and this, too, Luke flatly denies. On the other hand, there were Jewish Christians who demanded that Gentile Christians should obey all the demands of the law. Luke has both Paul and the leaders of the Jerusalem church reject this demand. It is possible, but not likely, that Luke saw the acceptance of the apostolic decree as being, in effect, acceptance of the Gentiles' partial obedience to the law. But his conclusion seems to be that while Jewish Christians may keep the law Gentile Christians need not. With respect to this debate between Jews, Jewish Christians, and Gentiles, not a word is spoken in the Pastorals. There the issue is quite different—in what sense is the law good for Christians in general, regardless of their origin? The answer given is that it is to be understood primarily in an ethical sense and, at least on one reading of 1 Tim. 1.6–10, is irrelevant to Christians who lead an upright life. A similar contrast is to be found in the attitude of Luke and the Pastor towards the Scriptures. For Luke the Old Testament is primarily a series of promises and prophecies which point forward to the era of Christ and his Church. Luke turns to the Old Testament to explain ostensibly strange or controversial events. In using the Old Testament in this way Luke clearly seems to be indicating one way in which the Church can appropriate the Old Testament. The Pastorals, on the other hand, understand the Old Testament primarily as a textbook of ethics. Gone is the grand scheme of promise and fulfilment, rooted as it is in a profound conviction of divine control over events, and in its place we find a pragmatic, down-to-earth use of the Scriptures. Is it conceivable that the same man could have been responsible for both views? I believe it is. Furthermore, I think a credible explanation can be given for these different emphases if we bring two factors to bear on the problem: first, the difference in genre and subject-matter between Luke–Acts and the Pastorals; and second, the different problems faced by the author when he wrote them.

Luke–Acts are indisputably narratives about past events. Whatever motivations one ascribes to Luke and however one assesses his reliability, there can be little doubt that he was trying to tell the story of Jesus and the Church. The Pastorals, on the other hand, are letters written not to describe past problems of the Church but to confront pressing issues in the present. This simple observation opens up one level of explanation for their differences. For one might argue that Luke could scarcely have written Acts without broaching the theme of Jews, Gentiles, and the law, whereas the absence of this theme from the Pastorals is wholly understandable. Likewise, one might argue that the presentation of the Old Testament within the scheme of promise and fulfilment is no more than a reflection of precisely those debates which took place between the early Church and the Jews, both using the same book as their Scriptures and both claiming to know its true meaning. This, it might be said, is why those who were faced with the 'proof from prophecy' argument were, in most cases, non-believing Jews whom the Church was attempting to convince. Finally, one might add, the story of Acts is primarily about the broad sweep of the Church's mission and not about the detailed problems of individual communities. The Pastorals, on the other hand, are addressed to individual communities (via their leaders) and the problems they faced. There was no need to convince them by 'proof from prophecy' for they were already convinced. Conversely, it would not have made much sense for the early Church to harp on the ethical value of the law, when their audience already accepted this but did not accept their basic kerygma! This line of reasoning can, I think, take us part of the way towards an explanation; but we must go further and consider the different situations in which these documents were produced.

There is no agreement on the *Sitz im Leben* of Acts or the purpose of Luke in writing it. In this context it is essential for us to decide only why Luke wrote about the law and used the Old Testament in the way he did, though this will clearly affect an account of his overall purpose. It is widely accepted that when Luke wrote Acts there was no active mission to the Jews. J. Jervell has argued that Acts was written for a community of Jewish–Christian stamp, in which the Jewish Christians were 'a respected and influential element'. Luke's purpose was both to oppose Jewish calumnies about Christianity, especially those directed at Paul, and at the same time to explain why there was no longer a Jewish mission and how Jewish and Gentile Christians should perceive their respective roles in the true Israel. Luke, he thinks, was making an important theological point: believing Jews are the true (not the new) Israel and unbelieving Jews have cut themselves off from the people of God; Gentiles participate in the blessing of Israel only by being grafted onto the people of God. I have argued elsewhere that I am not convinced by Jervell's interpretation of the relationship between Jewish and Gentile missions, any more than I am by his application of the same interpretation of Lucan theology to themes like the law, James, and Paul's apologetic speeches.[22] On the other hand, as well as giving us a highly original and provocative interpretation of Lucan theology he has, I think, also given us some valuable suggestions about the *Sitz im Leben* of Acts. Luke's account of Paul, and his consideration of law and Scripture, Jews and Gentiles, do indicate that one of the pressing problems facing Luke and his contemporaries was either Jewish or Jewish–Christian accusations. The attacks were probably directed not only against the Church in general but against Paul in particular. He was the leading figure in Gentile Christianity and it may well have been that the legitimacy of predominantly Gentile

Christian communities was questioned in the form of personal attacks on Paul—accusing him of being an enemy of the law, an apostate Jew and a renegade from the people of God. The *kerygmata Petrou* gives a vivid portrait of precisely this kind of accusation in its extreme form. It would, of course, be rash to connect this directly with the situation in which Luke wrote Acts, but it does illustrate the kind of anti-Pauline polemic that could arise among Jewish–Christian extremists, and it is not difficult to suppose that non-Christian Jews could have used similar arguments. It is difficult to surmise whether Luke was responding to Jewish or Jewish–Christian calumny.[23] In Acts, Paul is attacked both by Jews and by some Jewish Christians, but we need not assume that an identical situation prevailed at the time of writing. Nor does this necessarily indicate, as Jervell supposes, that Luke writes in a primarily Jewish–Christian milieu. On the contrary, I think it more probable that the Gentiles dominated the churches and that the Jews were, at the most, a respected minority. It is clear from Acts that if Luke was addressing non-Christian Jews he was engaged more in polemic than debate. The regular, pejorative references to 'the Jews' and their obduracy would scarcely have been received as sweet reason!

It is more likely that, whatever the origin of the debate over Jews and Gentiles in general and Paul in particular, Luke's reply is addressed to Christian communities. His reply to the accusation that both Paul and the churches he founded were an illegitimate offspring of Judaism is not primarily the theological notion that the Church is indeed the true Israel. His explanation is simpler: the present state of affairs is the result of the direct, miraculous intervention of God in history. What God initiated, encouraged, and confirmed was, moreover, no more than an expression of his eternal will as expressed in the Old Testament. On a practical level this does not mean that Jews who become Christians should cease to be Jews, any more than Gentiles who become Christians should cease to be Gentiles. The gospel comes to them in the situation they are in, building on, but at the same time correcting and redirecting, their pre-Christian piety. Thus it seems to me that Luke's attitude towards the law and Scripture in part grows out of the particular situation of the Lucan church.

Behind the Pastorals, however, lies a quite different problem. While there is no longer any dispute about the relative rights of

Jews and Gentiles, there is still disagreement about the correct understanding of the Old Testament and the figure of Paul. But the issues are quite different. It is no longer a case of a Christian versus a Jewish interpretation of the Old Testament, nor of a defence of Paul against his detractors. On the contrary, both the author and his opponents have a high regard for both: they both value the Old Testament, but want to use it in different ways; and they both value Paul, but cannot agree on the correct interpretation of his teaching. As we have suggested earlier, the Pastor seems to be opposing Jewish–Christian gnostics who argued that their speculative mythologies and ascetic demands were based on the Old Testament. At the same time they claimed Paul as their authority by disseminating their own interpretation of his writings or of oral traditions connected with him or, perhaps, by claiming to possess secret Pauline traditions. In these circumstances it would scarcely have been relevant to have written at some length about Jewish or Gentile–Christian observance of the law any more than it would have been for Luke to have written about the moral as opposed to the speculative use of the law. Likewise, while to write about the theme of Scripture as promise and fulfilment was relevant to both the subject-matter and *Sitz im Leben* of Luke–Acts, it would not have been relevant to the *Sitz im Leben* of the Pastorals. The same argument can explain one other feature of the Pastorals. In contrast to Luke–Acts the Pastorals make surprisingly little use of the Old Testament. In a situation where considerable interest in a speculative, mythological interpretation of the Old Testament was being engendered, it might have seemed wise not to make excessive use of Old Testament quotations since they would have been open to more than one interpretation![24] Instead he makes do with some firm statements about the non-speculative, pragmatic use of the Old Testament and confirms this with the occasional quotation or allusion.

It seems fair to conclude, therefore, that while the attitude towards law and Scripture in Luke–Acts and the Pastorals is not identical, neither is there any formal contradiction between them. The differences are, I would argue, differences of emphasis which result from the different genre, subject-matter, and *Sitz im Leben*. It is quite conceivable that the same man wrote both.

9

The Portrait of Paul

We turn now to a crucial theme for our discussion, not only because it illustrates important common perspectives, but also because it raises the most significant objections to the hypothesis of common authorship. N. Brox,[1] for example, correctly notes that one of the major difficulties of this thesis is the apparent divergence between the portrait of Paul in Acts and in the Pastorals. In this respect Brox represents the almost universal view that the Pastor did not know Acts, since his picture of Paul is so different. This is based on two main observations: first, that whereas in the Pastorals Paul is *the* apostle, in Acts he is not considered to be an apostle at all; and second, that the setting of each epistle in general, and the movements of Paul and his companions in particular, cannot be harmonized with the narrative of Acts. This chapter will deal only with the first of these issues, while the following chapter will address the second. We shall consider the image of Paul under three aspects: conversion, suffering and martyrdom, and apostleship.

PAUL'S CONVERSION

The allusions to Paul's conversion in the Pastorals, especially 1 Tim. 1.12–17, do not concern themselves with psychological explanations of that event; rather, they are theocentrically orient-ated. They do contrast the pre-Christian and Christian periods of Paul's career, but they do so in order to emphasize the gracious activity of God and not to pry into the mental state of Paul. In this they are in accord with both Acts and the Pauline epistles.

The only reference to Paul's pre-Christian life in the Pastorals is found in 1 Tim. 1.13:

> I formerly blasphemed and persecuted and insulted (*blasphemon kai diokten kai hubristen*) him; but I received mercy because I had acted ignorantly in unbelief.

Two observations are made here about Paul's pre-Christian career: first, that he was an enemy and persecutor of God and the Church; and second, that these actions were excused on the grounds of ignorance. That Paul persecuted the Church, and thus indirectly Christ himself (cf. Acts 9.4), is indisputable. It is confirmed both by Paul himself (1 Cor. 15.9; Phil. 3.5 f; Gal. 1.13 f) and by Luke (Acts 8.3; 9.1–2, 13–14, 21; 22.4–5; 26.11). It has been suggested, however, that the other two terms (*blasphemos*, *hubristes*) convey a different picture from both Paul and Acts. Thus G. Klein argues that *blasphemos* is used in 1 Tim. 1.13 in a general, unqualified sense akin to 1 Tim. 6.4; Tit. 3.2, and is not parallel to Acts 26.11 where Paul tries to force Christians to blaspheme.[2] It may be true, as many have suggested, that the terms were suggested to the Pastor by the catalogue of vices, but it is also clear that in 1 Tim. 1.13 the blasphemy is directed against Christ. In this respect the better parallels are 1 Tim. 1.20; 6.1, and Tit. 3.5, rather than the more general use in 1 Tim. 6.4; Tit. 3.2—if, indeed, such a distinction is valid. G. Kittel, for example, notes that even in the conventional vice-catalogues 'a predominantly religious connotation is present even when it is not expressed'.[3] Acts 26.11, therefore, is a valid parallel to 1 Tim. 1.13. The second term (*hubristes*) is found elsewhere in the New Testament only in Rom. 1.30, but it is not essentially different from the vivid descriptions of Paul's persecuting activity in Acts. The use of ignorance as a mitigating factor in the evaluation of Paul's pre-Christian activities finds close parallels in Acts. With respect to both Jews (Acts 3.17, cf. Luke 23.34; Acts 13.27) and Gentiles (Acts 17.30), ignorance is also used as a partial excuse for the behaviour of non-believers.[4] There is no direct parallel to 1 Tim. 1.13 in Luke's description of Paul's pre-Christian career, but since he (alone in the rest of the New Testament) uses the concept elsewhere, a statement such as 1 Tim. 1.13 is consonant with Lucan authorship. In their description of Paul's pre-Christian activity and their use of ignorance as an excuse, Luke and the Pastor can thus be seen to be in harmony.

Their agreement is the more marked when we contrast what they say with Paul's own statements. Thus it is often observed that of the three terms used in 1 Tim. 1.13 only 'persecutor' fits Paul's specific case and that, in view of Phil. 3.4 f, 'it is inconceivable that Paul would have used *blasphemos* or *hubristes* of his own past'.[5]

The use in 1 Tim. 1.13 of ignorance as a partial excuse does not preclude an emphasis on divine grace nor does it imply sinlessness, and it is not inconceivable that Paul could have written it; however, since it is open to such a misinterpretation, it is unlikely that it was written by Paul.[6] Finally, we may note that the statement in 1 Tim. 1.15 that Paul is the foremost (*protos*) of sinners, whether it is taken to mean 'first' or 'greatest', is unlikely to have been made by Paul, but is conceivable as a Lucan assertion. It is remarkable, therefore, that while the statements in 1 Tim. 1.13 f do not recall Paul's own statements, they are essentially in accord with Acts.

The allusion to Paul's conversion in 1 Tim. 1.12–17 has two main features. First, since he has been portrayed as the foremost of sinners (v. 16) his conversion becomes an example, or perhaps even a prototype (v. 17 *hupotuposis* is ambiguous), of Christian conversion. Second, in making this point, the Pastor vividly contrasts the two periods of Paul's life. His pre-Christian past stands in dramatic contrast to his Christian present. Both of these features in 1 Tim. 1.12–17 contribute to the end-product—a stylized, ideal portrait of Paul, a man whose conversion is both a model and a source of hope for all non-believers. The perspective is unmistakably post-Pauline, offering a retrospective assessment of Paul's dramatic turnabout and using it for parenetic purposes.

While this perspective on Paul's conversion is not found in his own writings, it is found in Acts. The description of Paul's conversion there clearly makes use of the 'contrast-effect'. The vivid descriptions of Paul's persecution activity in Acts 9, 22, 26, where it is described in progressively more violent terms, is designed to dramatize the subsequent conversion and emphasize its miraculous nature.[7] In one dramatic move, as a result of divine intervention, the chief persecutor becomes the chief missionary of the Church. Moreover, while there is no direct statement to the effect that Luke views Paul's conversion as exemplary or archetypal, it can scarcely be doubted that this is one of his motives in repeating the account three times and at some length. That this is not specifically stated in Acts, and that other themes such as the importance of this event in the history of the early Church do not appear in the Pastorals, is to be expected given the difference in subject-matter, purpose and genre. Similarly, while it is true that in Acts the accounts of Paul's pre-Christian activities and conversion are far more detailed, this is chiefly because of the narrative form. One would not expect such details in an epistolary setting.

It is reasonable to conclude, therefore, that Luke and the Pastor not only agree with each other but diverge from Paul. Both give fundamentally the same post-Pauline view of Paul's conversion and pre-Christian life. There is nothing which contradicts the theory of common authorship, and much to recommend it. It is perhaps worth adding that it has often been suggested that the faithful saying in 1 Tim. 1.15, 'Christ Jesus came into the world to save sinners', is based on Luke 19.10, 'The Son of man came to seek and to save the lost'. And if there is no direct connection, it remains true that Luke 19.10 is the closest parallel to 1 Tim. 1.15.

PAUL'S SUFFERING AND MARTYRDOM

One of the most consistent features of the portrait of Paul in the Pastorals is the image of him as a deserted, persecuted apostle, suffering for his faith and, according to 2 Timothy, conscious that his martyrdom was both inevitable and imminent. The whole of 2 Timothy is suffused with this theme, but it is shown most clearly in 1.3–18; 2.9–10; 3.10–13; 4.6–22.

In 2 Timothy Paul is described as a deserted and lonely figure. Timothy, his close and beloved companion, had previously departed 'with many tears' (2 Tim. 2.4)—an allusion which some would place historically at Acts 20.37.[8] Paul mentions that he longs to see Timothy again (2 Tim. 1.4) and asks him to come soon (2 Tim. 4.9). In addition, most of his other close companions are scattered far and wide (2 Tim. 4.10 f) and Luke alone is with him (2 Tim. 4.11).[9] At an earlier stage Onesiphorus had made a great effort to visit Paul (2 Tim. 1.16–18), but many of the Asians, including Hermogenes and Phygelus, had deliberately denied him (2 Tim. 1.15) and he poignantly observes that during his 'first defence' everyone deserted him (2 Tim. 4.16).

In addition to Paul's sense of loneliness and desertion, the Pastor repeatedly emphasizes his sufferings as a Christian. His appointment by God to be an apostle, preacher, and teacher necessarily involves suffering (2 Tim. 1.11–12; 2.9; 3.11). This suffering accompanies his whole career (2 Tim. 3.11), but is brought to a climax by his imprisonment (2 Tim. 1.6; 2.9). That this suffering is neither fortuitous nor associated solely with Paul is indicated in 2 Tim. 3.12, 'Indeed all who desire to live a godly life in Christ Jesus will be persecuted', and in 2 Tim. 1.8, 23 where Timothy is exhorted to 'take your share of the suffering for the gospel . . .'.

Finally, in 2 Tim. 4.6 f, Paul views his imminent death with remarkable equanimity. He has 'fought the good fight' and 'kept the faith', so he can be proud of his past as he looks back. His future lies with the Lord who will now, as before, 'rescue him from all evil' and ensure his salvation (2 Tim. 1.18) and due reward (2 Tim. 1.8). It appears that he had already undergone an earlier hearing or trial and had been able to turn the tables on his captors by preaching to the Gentiles. If the reference is to an earlier trial and subsequent period of freedom, then this preaching presumably refers to the continuing Gentile mission; if it refers to the first of two hearings then the preaching was presumably in court, in front of his accusers and judges. Either way, 'that the preaching of the chief apostle to the Gentiles should find its climax in a trial situation exemplifies the view of the whole epistle—i.e., that persecution and suffering are an integral part of the preaching of the word'.[10]

How does the Pastor understand this aspect of Paul's career? Primarily, Paul is being presented as a paradigm for Christian believers. In the same way that his conversion is seen as an example, so is his whole career. He is the archetypal faithful steward of the gospel—persecuted and finally martyred for his faith, but firm in his commitment to the end. As 2 Tim. 1.8; 3.12 (and 2.11?) make clear, what happens to Paul exemplifies the fate of all believers. It has often been assumed on this basis, probably correctly, that the recipients of the Pastorals were themselves undergoing persecution. It is possible, too, that the Pastor goes beyond seeing Paul as a mere example:

> Therefore I endure everything for the sake of the elect, that they also may obtain the salvation which in Christ Jesus goes with eternal glory (2 Tim. 2.10).

It might be argued that this recalls the notoriously obscure verse in Col. 1.24, where Paul seems to claim that his suffering is in some sense vicarious, endured on behalf of his brethren and completing the suffering of Christ.[11] However, the notion of a fixed amount of suffering prior to the end, which probably lies behind Col. 1.24, is not even hinted at in 2 Tim. 2.10, nor is it clear that Paul's suffering is vicarious.[12]

With respect to Paul's suffering and persecutions, Acts, like the Pauline epistles, offers many parallels. He was persecuted by the Hellenists in Jerusalem (Acts 9.29), perpetually harassed by the Jews (Acts 13.50; 14.2, 5, 19; 16.19–24; 17.5–9; 18.6, 12 f; 21—24), assaulted by Artemis-worshippers (Acts 18.23 f) and finally taken into custody by the Romans (Acts 24—28). Moreover, the suffering is seen by Luke to be an integral part of Paul's divinely designated role as chief missionary to the Gentiles, and is declared to be such at his conversion (Acts 9.16; 26.21). When speaking to the Ephesian elders Paul himself intimates that suffering is a concomitant of the Christian ministry (Acts 20.19, 23–4). And Acts, like the Pastorals, recognizes that Paul's suffering and imprisonment do not hinder the spread of the gospel (2 Tim. 2.9; Acts 28.30–1), for in both there is an overriding sense of divine control.

There is no direct parallel to 2 Tim. 4.6 f in Acts, since Acts 28 tells us almost nothing about his imprisonment. There are hints earlier in the book, however, which suggest a similar outlook on Paul's death. The review of his past career in which he claims to have 'run the race' and 'fought the fight' recalls not only the specific use of the same metaphor in Acts 20.24, but also the general tenor of Acts 20.19–23. It is in this same speech that we get one of the few allusions in Acts to Paul's ultimate fate (Acts 20.24–5, 38, cf. 21.10–14). However, apart from these few allusions, there is no description of Paul's ultimate fate even though, presumably, it was known to both author and readers. The ending of Acts is, of course, one of the book's greatest enigmas, for Luke concludes with a vague reference to Paul's two-year house arrest in Rome, which allowed him unhindered preaching of the gospel (Acts 28.30–1). The image of the lonely, deserted apostle facing imminent martyrdom would thus have to be considered as an addition to the information in Acts. Of course, 2 Timothy does not describe Paul's death any more than Acts does, but that is inevitable in an epistle ascribed to Paul!

However, it is important to note that this is not a substantial discrepancy. If the Pastor either knew or believed that Paul was released after his two-year detention and that his death came at a later stage, there would be no contradiction with 2 Timothy. If, on the other hand, he located 2 Timothy during the imprisonment in Acts 28, the difference becomes explicable if one allows for the different purpose in each case. Acts 28 is the climax of a narrative which is concerned more to convey a sense of the triumphal progress of the gospel from Jerusalem to the ends of the earth (Acts 1.8) than it is with the fate of the individual Paul, and more with a general statement about his last two years than with a detailed description of his last few months. There is no difficulty in supposing that the author of 2 Timothy 4.9 f understood it to be a description of Paul's circumstances at the end of his two-year detention mentioned in Acts 28. Indeed, it may be that 2 Timothy confirms a recent explanation for the enigmatic ending of Acts. C. K. Barrett suggests that Acts ends where it does because 'an account of the martyrdom itself, especially if at that time Paul was deserted by his friends and the victim of some kind of treachery, would not enhance the record of Paul's devotion and might detract from the sense of confidence, victory and unity that pervade the book.'[13] It may be precisely such a situation which Luke, writing at a later date and for a different purpose, hints at in 2 Tim. 1.15; 4.9 f. It is not clear exactly what 2 Tim. 1.15 refers to, but it could be that 'all those in Asia' not only 'turned away' from Paul, but also conspired in his imprisonment and death. 2 Tim. 4.9 f refers to the desertion of Paul by most of his travelling companions and v. 16 claims that 'at my first defence no one took my part; all deserted me'. Is it possible that this reflects what Luke knew when he wrote Acts, namely that there were Christians who had a hand in his death, either by positive action or passive compliance? Paul's death could not, of course, be narrated in 2 Timothy, but Luke took the opportunity to use the picture of Paul as the deserted, lonely, suffering apostle to good effect. It would have made a poignant but anticlimactic ending to the narrative of Acts, but in 2 Timothy it enhances the idealized portrait of Paul as the archetypal Christian believer who holds firmly to his faith whatever befalls him.

C. H. Talbert has suggested that the portraits of Jesus, Stephen, and Paul in the Lucan writings are used as an anti-gnostic device. In particular, he argues that Luke rejects the connection between Jesus' death and the forgiveness of sins, and portrays it instead as the death of an innocent martyr. The purpose is to counter the view of those gnostics who rejected martyrdom on principle (Iren.,

Adv. Haer. XXXIV, 3–6; Tert., *Adv. Haer.* I).[14] It will be argued below that this is not the most probable setting for Acts, though it is for the Pastorals. One might argue, therefore, that the portrait of Paul in 2 Timothy *is* motivated by the gnostic refusal of martyrdom and, in turn, this is one reason why there are more specific allusions to Paul's martyrdom in 2 Timothy than in Acts.

It is scarcely in dispute, however, that Luke thought Paul's career was of central and exemplary significance. It is clear that whatever historical or antiquarian interests he may have had, he was also telling his story with an eye on his contemporaries and their needs. Thus while the account of Paul may serve several functions (historical, polemical, etc.), one of these is to present his life as a paradigm. There is a message for the readers of Acts not only in the teaching of the apostles but also in the way they lived. There is no hint that Paul's suffering was vicarious, but then such a notion cannot definitely be found in 2 Timothy either. In general, the information which Luke and the Pastor provide on Paul's suffering and death is consistent. There are many similarities, and where 2 Timothy gives additional information it is always consistent with the narrative of Acts.

PAUL AS APOSTLE

It has been asserted that when the Pastorals single Paul out as *the* apostle, the sole guardian of the truth and source of sound teaching, they contradict not only Acts, where the apostles are the Twelve and Paul is simply one link in the chain of tradition, but also those genuine epistles where Paul recognizes his dependence on his predecessors.[15] There are two issues at stake: first, the use of the word 'apostle'; and second, the exclusive concentration on the figure of Paul in the Pastorals.

It is significant that the Pastorals seldom use the word apostle. It occurs five times, of which three are in the standard introductory formula of each epistle (1 Tim. 1.1; 2 Tim. 1.1; Tit. 1.1). The use in 2 Tim. 1.11 is not particularly emphatic: 'For this gospel I was appointed a preacher and apostle and teacher'. The title apostle is used as one of several ways in which Paul's role is described. A similar statement in 1 Tim. 2.7 connects 'apostle' and 'preacher', but here there is also a firm parenthetical affirmation—'I am telling the truth, I am not lying'. The formulaic uses at the beginning of each epistle are predictable if, as seems likely, the author knew at least some of the genuine Pauline epistles (Rom. 1.1; 1 Cor. 1.1; 2 Cor. 1.1; Gal. 1.1; Col. 1.1, etc.). The same can be said of 1 Tim. 2.7, since in Rom. 9.1; 2 Cor. 11.31; Gal. 1.20 Paul makes similar affirmations. On a formal level it is scarcely appropriate in a personal letter to Timothy, who would need no such reassurance, but it may be that some in Ephesus did. It is more likely, however, that this is one of the many instances where the genuine Pauline letters have influenced the wording of the Pastorals. It is noticeable, therefore, that apart from 1 Tim. 2.7 there is little emphasis on the title apostle as such. Certainly, when it does occur it is always with reference to Paul. But this is not because there is any desire to belittle the Twelve or any others who traditionally bore the title; it is part of the broader problem of the exclusive concentration on the figure of Paul in the Pastorals, and it is to this that we now turn.

The Pastorals unambiguously portray Paul as the sole source of genuine tradition and, by implication, assert that Timothy and Titus and any successors they appoint are those who preserve this tradition. This is clear in the format of the letters which are addressed by Paul to his companions Timothy and Titus and which contain instructions both for them and for the communities they oversee (1 Tim. 1.18; 3.14; 4.6, 11; 5.21; 6.2, 11, 14; 2 Tim. 1.6; 2.14; 3.14; 4.1; Tit. 1.5; 2.1, 15; 3.8). More specifically, 1 Tim. 6.20; 2 Tim. 1.12–14 speak of the deposit (*paratheke*) which has been entrusted to Paul, which he entrusts to Timothy, and Timothy is to entrust to his successors (2 Tim. 2.2). It is, therefore, Paul above all who is the source of sound teaching and truth for the communities to whom the Pastorals are addressed.

The information in Acts is more ambiguous. With respect to the title apostle, it is usually concluded that Acts differs not only from the Pastorals but from Paul. The key passages for our argument are Acts 14.4, 14, since it is only here that Luke attributes the title to Paul (cf. Acts 1.21–2 which ostensibly give the qualifications for apostleship). I have argued elsewhere that the various attempts to show that Acts 14.4, 14 do not represent, or perhaps even contradict, Luke's view of apostleship are not persuasive.[16] Whatever one makes of these verses it seems that at the very least they indicate that Luke did not have a rigid conception which confined the title

to the Twelve and that he had no objection to its application to
Paul (and Barnabas). Perhaps he believed it was originally confined to the Twelve and later used more widely. Or perhaps he
believed that Paul and Barnabas were not apostles in the same
sense as the Twelve, but for historical and not dogmatic reasons—
the Twelve had a unique and unrepeatable function: 'Their (Paul
and Barnabas) apostolic task was not to found and care for the
infant church in its initial stages of growth for they were later
converts. Nevertheless, because they founded and cared for
churches in the initial stages of the Gentile mission, they were
equally apostles'.[17] However one explains them, if one thinks Luke
wrote the Pastorals, Acts 14.4, 14 undoubtedly give a precedent
for the application of the title apostle to Paul in those letters.[18]

Acts provides a more complete picture of Paul's position within
Christian tradition than the Pastorals, since there is a considerable
amount of information about his relationship with his predecessors
as well as his successors. This double aspect of Paul's work has
been most thoroughly discussed by G. Klein. He argues that while
Paul is wholly subordinated to his predecessors, he has absolute
authority over his successors.[19] His conclusions are, I think, too
rigid and they break down at several crucial points in the narrative
of Acts. Thus he argues that Acts 13.1 f narrates the legitimizing
of Paul's transformation from subordinate to leader, the church
at Antioch already having been legitimized by the Twelve. But
since the agent of that legitimization was Barnabas (Acts 11.22 f).
it is curious that the church at Antioch should be commissioning
him as well as Paul! Klein observes but does not successfully
answer this objection. Similarly, his attempt to find significance
in the changing order in which Paul and Barnabas are mentioned
as a pair puts an unwarranted strain upon the text. It is surely no
more than a literary variation, of which Luke is fond, and is
without theological significance. Despite this, there is some substance to Klein's observations. It is clear that Luke attaches Paul
closely to the original Christian community in Jerusalem. He meets
the Twelve soon after his conversion (Acts 9.26–30), ends each
journey in Jerusalem (Acts 15.2; 18.22; 21.17), is assigned by the
church at Antioch to represent them on the Gentile issue in
Jerusalem (Acts 15.1 f), and accepts the decisions of the apostles
and elders (Acts 16.4). However, it is also clear that there is no
attempt to subordinate Paul to the Twelve or the Jerusalem

church. His conversion is an independent event, since Ananias is not seen as the representative of the Twelve.[20] He is commissioned by the church at Antioch (Acts 13.1 f) and his dealings with the church in Jerusalem are as much with the elders and James (Acts 15.22; 21.18) as with the Twelve. Thus while Paul clearly has a close and amicable relationship with the Jerusalem church, he is not subordinated to them any more than he is to the church at Antioch.

With respect to his successors, the information in Acts accords well with the Pastorals. Acts 14.23 reports that Paul and Barnabas appointed elders in the new churches they had founded. According to Acts 19.1–7, Paul has authority over those who know only the baptism of John and is the means whereby they receive the Spirit. It is, however, to Acts 20.17–33 that we must turn for the most complete picture. In a speech which in both form and content is unique in Acts, Paul bids farewell to the Ephesian elders. It is his only speech to Christian leaders and, like the speech to the Gentiles in Acts 17.22 f, is clearly intended to be archetypal. It is an idealized scene, where Paul takes leave not only of the Ephesian elders but of all church officials and congregations. Moreover, this speech affords one of the most remarkable parallels to the Pastorals, in particular to 2 Timothy. The similarity goes far beyond the observation that they are both examples of a particular literary genre, the farewell speech.[21] Almost every detail of Acts 20.17–33 can be found in the Pastorals.[22]

1 Paul looks back on his past career with some confidence, believing that he has fulfilled the tasks designated for him (Acts 20.18–21, 25–6; 2 Tim. 4.6 f). Moreover, the striking metaphor of an athlete finishing his race is used in both Acts 20.24 (*hos teleioso ton dromon mou*) and 2 Tim. 4.7 (*ton dromon teteleka*). At the same time he is deeply concerned with the fate of the Church in his absence. This is indicated by the whole of Acts 20.17–35 and each of the Pastoral letters.

2 The problem Paul foresees and warns of is heresy, which will assault the Church from within and without (Acts 20.29–30; 1 Tim. 1.3 f; 3.1 f; 6.20 f; 2 Tim. 2.14 f; 3.1 f). The heresy appears to be an early form of gnosticism and its centre is in Ephesus (Acts 20.17 f; 1 Tim. 1.3).[23] Paul urges constant alertness (Acts 20.31; 2 Tim. 4.2 f).

3   The responsibility for resisting the false teaching is placed on
the church leaders or on Paul's assistants. The church leaders are,
in both cases, elder-bishops (Acts 20.17–28; 1 Tim. 5.17; 2 Tim.
2.2; Tit. 1.5 f), and it is Paul's example and instruction which
will be their chief weapon (Acts 20.27, 30–5; 1 Tim. 3.14; 4.11 f;
6.20; 2 Tim. 1.8 f, 13–14; 3.10 f; Tit. 1.5).

4   Paul speaks of his own suffering for the sake of the gospel (Acts
20.19–24; 2 Tim. 1.11–12; 2.3; 3.11) and indicates that for him a
martyr's death lies ahead (Acts 20.25, 37; 2 Tim. 4.6 f).

5   The ministers whom Paul appoints and exhorts are warned of
the dangers of the love of money (Acts 20.33–5; 1 Tim. 6.9–10;
Tit. 1.11).

6   Paul commits his successors to the Lord and his grace (Acts
20.32; 2 Tim. 4.22).

How is this speech to be assessed within the context of Acts?
E. Haenchen suggests a variety of motives.[24] An obvious one is the
desire to present Paul as the archetypal Christian minister, the
prototype for later generations. This motive would, of course, be
fully in line with the Pastorals. Haenchen also suggests that, since
the churches in Asia Minor had succumbed to gnosticism soon
after Paul's death (Rev. 1—2), Luke wishes to absolve Paul from
any responsibility. Paul is blameless for he has not shrunk from
declaring anything to his successors. G. Klein more plausibly
suggests that a quite different motive was at work.[25] The problem
was not that Christians were accusing Paul of failure, but that the
gnostics were claiming Paul as the authority for their teaching. The
speech asserts that, despite their claim that Paul is their authority,
in reality they are excluded from the genuine Pauline tradition and
do not have the Pauline 'deposit'. The repeated claim that Paul
has withheld nothing from the elders (Acts 20.27, 30, 35) is not a
claim of innocence, but an assertion that Paul's appointed
successors alone have his true teaching, and they have all of it.
There is only one Pauline tradition, so that any claim to possess a
secret Pauline tradition is opposed by Paul himself!

On this note we can now turn to a consideration of some of the
explanations of the similarities and differences between the
portrait of Paul in Luke–Acts and in the Pastorals. With particular
reference to Acts 20.17–35 W. Schmithals says, 'I consider the

speech to be a piece, reworked by Luke, of the so-called "itinerary", the author of which stood close to the author of the Pastorals or was even identical with him, though I cannot at this time more fully establish this assumption'.[26] It should be noted that Schmithals considers the Pastorals to be 'wholly non-Lucan' and ascribes the Pastorals and Luke–Acts to quite different Christian streams—the former to Gentile Hellenistic Christianity and the latter to Jewish Hellenistic Christianity. However, as I shall argue below, while Schmithals' observations confirm the similarity between this speech and the Pastorals he does not offer convincing evidence for the non-Lucan origin of Acts 20.17–35, nor does his observation account for the many similarities between Luke and the Pastor which lie outside the itinerary. N. Brox offers a broader explanation for this phenomenon.[27] He suggests that the Pastor drew on a variety of Pauline traditions that were preserved in both written and oral form by his successors and supporters. The Lucan traditions were one among many sources which the Pastor used. This is a possible explanation but, in my view, does not go far enough. C. H. Talbert suggests that the similarities between Acts and the Pastorals, especially those between Acts 20.17–35 and 2 Timothy, are because both Luke and the Pastor were combating gnosticism.[28] This is, of course, part of his overall thesis that Luke and Acts are primarily anti-gnostic documents. This does not seem to me, however, to be the most probable explanation of the purpose of Luke's writings, and especially of Acts.

In the course of arguing for Lucan influence on the Pastorals A. Strobel[29] offers a curious explanation for Acts 20.17–35. Commenting in particular on the use of the same athletic metaphor in Acts 20.24 and 2 Tim. 4.7, he argues that the latter is neither a literary fiction nor a secondary construction based on Acts 20.24. Rather, when Luke wrote Acts 20.24, at a later date, he drew on his memory of the authentic words of Paul. He then notes that when 2 Tim. 4.12 indicates that a short time beforehand Tychicus had been sent to Ephesus, this was probably to convey a message similar to Acts 20 and possibly also to deliver 1 Timothy. This is a puzzling series of statements,[30] not least because Strobel nowhere else discusses exactly what he means by Lucan 'authorship' of the Pastorals or how he views the chronological relationship between the Lucan writings and the Pastorals. All we have are a few obscure and confusing hints. If he is implying that 2 Timothy (and 1 Timothy?) are Pauline this contradicts his own attempt to show that they are 'Lucan'. The appeal to the sending of Tychicus in 2 Tim. 4.12 is presumably meant to suggest that 2 Timothy was, like 1 Timothy, written to Timothy while he was in Ephesus, thus forging a connection with Paul's farewell address to the Ephesian elders. He seems to be implying that Luke was Paul's companion, that he wrote Acts after the Pastorals, and that Acts was based in part on his first-hand knowledge of Paul's activities. One must assume then that he thinks Luke was Paul's scribe, and that the Pastorals are a mixture of Pauline dictation and Lucan transcription. In other words, his explanation of the relationship would be the same as Moule's.[31] Valuable as Strobel's article is in drawing attention to the many similarities between Luke and the Pastor, his obscurity at the crucial stage of explanation does not enhance the defence of common authorship.

Both the similarities and differences in the portrait of Paul seem to require a different explanation from those considered above. The nub of the problem is this: if Luke wrote the Pastorals why, in those letters, is the title apostle confined to Paul and why is exclusive attention paid to him at the expense of his predecessors in the Christian tradition? If one accepts that Acts provides precedents for the application of the title apostle to Paul, then it should be remembered that we are dealing here not so much with a contradiction as with a difference of emphasis. The emphasis on Paul's relationship with his successors and the description of it are the same in Acts and the Pastorals. It is the omission of any reference to his predecessors and the resulting concentration on Paul in the Pastorals which is different from Acts. One level of explanation could be as follows: Luke reconstructed Paul's career as best he could, given the limitations of his sources and his own predispositions, but without any polemical purpose. Since he was intent on writing an account of the expansion of the Church he had to write about Paul and about Paul's predecessors and his dealings with them, for they were an integral part of the story. Consideration of them is forced upon Luke by the historical realities of his chosen subject-matter. On the other hand, if he wrote the Pastorals too, though in the name of Paul, the question of predecessors did not arise any more than it did in every genuine Pauline epistle. There the issue arises only for specific reasons related to the situation of the community to which it is addressed. Moreover, concentration on the figure of Paul can be explained in large part precisely because the letters are written in Paul's name, as against Acts where both the stage and the number of players are far larger. Such an explanation of the differences may be a partial answer to the problem; but there is another level of argument yet to be pursued.

The portrait in Acts of Paul in particular and the Gentile mission in general appears to be motivated in part by problems facing the communities for which Luke wrote. In particular they suggest that these were Gentile communities founded by Paul, but were located in a predominantly Jewish environment.[32] It is probable that these communities were under attack by Jews or Jewish Christians who accused them of apostasy, directing the attack in particular at their founder, Paul.

The Pastorals, on the other hand, were written in the face of a quite different threat both to Paul and to the Church. The threat came from gnostic enthusiasts who infiltrated the churches in a more subtle manner: they did not attack Paul; on the contrary, they used him. For it was to Paul and his writings that they appealed as the basis for their teaching. N. Brox has argued convincingly that the Pastorals are not an attempt to rehabilitate Paul for the Church as a result of misuse of his views by gnostics, as if the letters are intended to authenticate the author; rather, it is the teaching of the Pastorals, the genuine Pauline tradition, that is being authenticated by Paul.[33] That gnostics were active in Ephesus is indicated not only by Acts 20.17–35 and the Pastorals but also by Revelation 1—2, which speaks of the infiltration of the Nicolaitans into the churches of Asia Minor. That there were gnostics who used Paul's writings to support their views is indicated most clearly by 2 Pet. 3.15–16.

It is these two quite different situations, both intimately connected with the figure of Paul, which provide the most adequate explanation of the difference in emphasis between Acts and the Pastorals and which allow a defence of their common authorship. When he wrote Acts, Luke was faced primarily with an anti-Pauline opposition of a Jewish or Jewish–Christian character. This is why Paul's faithfulness to his Jewish heritage and his harmonious relationship with the Jerusalem church are emphasized. Luke is refuting those who argue that Paul is an apostate Jew, a renegade who had led his wing of the Church into heresy. Paul and the churches he founded remained true to their Jewish heritage and, ironically, if anything it was the obduracy of the Jews which precipitated the expansion into the Gentile world. On the other hand, when he wrote the Pastorals the problem was quite different. The opposition was now pro-Pauline. They claimed Paul as their chief authority and bolstered their case with reference to his own writings. In the face of this more subtle assault on Paul's teaching, there was no need to emphasize Paul's Jewishness or his relationship with his predecessors. The problem was with the tradition which came after, and in part emanated from, Paul. The crucial issue was, therefore, who had the true Pauline 'deposit' and how it was to be transmitted to subsequent generations. And thus the concentration is almost exclusively on the figure of Paul and his successors.

Perhaps a slightly modified version of this argument will serve my purpose as well. It could be argued that although the primary problem facing Luke when he wrote his account of Paul in Acts was anti-Paulinism, the inclusion of Acts 20.17–35 suggests that this was not the only problem. Likewise, while the Pastorals are almost wholly concerned with guaranteeing the preservation of the genuine Pauline tradition, there is at least in 1 Tim. 2.7 (cf. 1 Tim. 1.12–16; 2 Tim. 1.11) a modest but firm defence of Paul's rank as apostle. Perhaps the situation was as follows: when Luke wrote Acts anti-Paulinism was the major threat, but the gnostics had appeared on the horizon. They were not as yet a major influence but they clearly spelled trouble ahead, and Acts 20.17–35 is Luke's attempt to head them off before they became more influential. However, at a later date it was clear to Luke that the gnostics were becoming increasingly influential. They had not died a natural death nor had they been effectively countered. The number of their adherents was increasing and they had infiltrated many churches. What was worse, they used Paul's teaching as their authority and possibly some of his writings. In the face of this Luke returns to the task he had begun in Acts 20.17–35, but with two differences: first, he attacks them at much greater length and with more vehemence; and second, he counters their use of Pauline teaching by producing anti-gnostic writings in the name of Paul. At the same time there may still have been a few Jews or Jewish Christians who fired an occasional salvo at Paul and the communities he founded, reviving an earlier controversy. It is not the chief problem any longer, but it warrants a brief response (1 Tim. 2.7, etc.).[34]

This scenario may also be used to explain the slight shift of perspective which can be found between Acts and the Pastorals. In Acts 20.29 Paul warns that the heretics will be active 'after my departure (*meta ten aphixin mou*)'. This is often taken to mean that Paul is seen as the last of the great heroic figures in the heresy-free apostolic era. When he departs, heresy arrives.[35] Thus while he can foresee what will happen and warn his successors, he is not himself directly involved in the conflict. The Pastorals, on the other hand, place Paul in the thick of the battle.[36] If *aphixis* is given its usual meaning, 'arrival', the contrast would, of course, disappear. And if it is taken to mean 'departure' it could refer not to his death, but to his departure from Ephesus. This would be feasible even with the other allusions to Paul's death in the speech and even if one reads it as an ideal, paradigmatic scene. The Ephesian elders will not see Paul again, but as the narrative unfolds it becomes clear that his death is a few years off. If one imagines that Luke located the Pastorals chronologically in the period after the imprisonment of Acts 28 there would then be no problem. But if he located them within the narrative of Acts, and 1 Timothy and Titus to a period prior to Acts 20.17–35, then clearly he would have imagined Paul to be disputing with gnostics in Ephesus and Crete *before* his farewell speech to the Ephesian elders—and that would contradict either interpretation of Acts 20.29. We shall return to these chronological issues in the next chapter. A different, and perhaps more satisfactory argument, would be that Luke, writing a few years after he had completed Acts and faced with an urgent need to counter the gnostic threat, momentarily forgets the perspective of Acts 20. In his desire to introduce the voice of Paul into the dispute over who were the true interpreters of the Pauline tradition, he places Paul in the thick of the battle. Of course, even in the Pastorals Paul's involvement is indirect, in the form of epistles; he is not physically present in Ephesus or Crete. Moreover, there is also some oscillation between the prediction of future false teaching and the recognition that it is present (cf. 2 Tim. 3.1 f; 4.3 f). However one assesses this point, I think the shift of perspective, when seen in context, is not a serious objection to common authorship. Certainly, it is no more of an anomaly than some of the discrepancies we can certainly ascribe to Luke, such as the differences between the dating and description of the ascension in Luke 24 and Acts 1.

All in all, an analysis of the image of Paul in Acts and the Pastorals lends support to the hypothesis of common authorship. There are differences of emphasis, but they are the result in part of purely literary factors and in part of the different contexts in which the works were written. There are many similarities, the most striking of which is between Acts 20 and 2 Timothy. It is not only feasible, but likely, that Luke was the author of both.

10

Pauline Chronology

There is a widely accepted opinion that the chronological and biographical information in the Pastorals cannot be harmonized either with Acts or with the Pauline epistles. This view, of course, is usually discussed in connection with the problem of the Pauline authorship of the Pastorals. The hypothesis of Lucan authorship demands a similar discussion, especially with respect to Acts. However, the assumption that Luke, when he wrote the Pastorals, probably knew some of Paul's epistles and used some of his travel notes necessitates a comparison of the Pastorals with the Pauline epistles too. In general, the arguments for and against Pauline authorship apply equally well with respect to Lucan authorship, though some new factors are brought into play.

We shall first consider whether the Pastorals can be fitted into Paul's career as it is described in Acts, and at a later stage we shall consider the so-called second imprisonment theory. 1 Timothy and Titus offer little chronological information and can be discussed quite briefly. The relevant texts in 1 Timothy are as follows:

> As I urged you when I was going to Macedonia, remain at Ephesus. . . . (1.3)
>
> I hope to come to you soon (3.14, cf. 4.13).

These verses imply that Timothy, the recipient of the letter, is in Ephesus. Paul has probably been in Ephesus recently, but has now left for Macedonia. He is at liberty to plan his future movements and intends to return to Ephesus soon.

According to Acts, Paul was twice in Macedonia. On the first occasion (Acts 16.11 f) Timothy accompanied him and there is no indication that Paul had previously worked in Ephesus. The information in 1 Timothy, therefore, can scarcely be equated with Acts 16. The second visit of Paul to Macedonia, described in

Acts 21.1 f, can be harmonized with 1 Timothy if two assumptions
are made: first, that the original reading in Acts 20.5 was *proselthontes* rather than *proelthontes*; and second, that sometime after
Paul had sent him to Macedonia (Acts 19.22) Timothy had returned
to Ephesus. *Proselthontes* is probably the better reading[1] and the
variant can be explained as an attempt to harmonize Acts either
with the Corinthian correspondence or, more probably, with Acts
19.22. This would imply that Timothy was not in Greece with
Paul, but that he went from Ephesus to meet him in Troas. The
second assumption, of course, follows inevitably from the first. If
Timothy was in Ephesus (Acts 20.5) he must have returned from
his earlier trip to Macedonia (Acts 19.22). The lacuna between Acts
19.22 and 20.5 is not untypical of Luke, for his chronological
notices are often vague—sometimes no doubt because of the
fragmentary nature of his sources—and his interest is mainly in
Paul and not in his companions. We should probably consider this
to be an inadvertent mistake. The same applies when we look
beyond Acts 20.5, for although that verse might seem to imply that
all seven companions accompanied Paul from then on, only
Trophimus (Acts 21.29) and Aristarchus (Acts 27.2) are subsequently mentioned. It is clear, therefore, that Luke could have
considered Acts 20.1 f to be the setting for 1 Timothy and that it
would not have contradicted his earlier narrative.

A further possibility is that Luke, with the new information he
had gained from reading some of Paul's epistles, realized that his
earlier narrative was incomplete. In particular, reading 1 and 2
Corinthians, which in their original form may have consisted of at
least four letters and maybe more, he would have realized that
Paul's dealings with Corinth were far more complex than he had
suggested in Acts. 2 Cor. 12.14; 13.1 refer to Paul's third visit to
Corinth. If he equated Acts 18 with the first and Acts 20.2 with the
third, he would have known that Paul had paid at least one visit to
Corinth between these two (cf. 2 Cor. 1.15 f.), written letters to
them (1 Cor. 5.4; 2 Cor. 2.3 f; 7.8, etc.), and twice sent Titus
there (2 Cor. 2.12–13; 7.5 f; 8.16 f). Luke may then have assumed
that 1 Timothy was written during this period, perhaps when Paul
went to meet Titus in Macedonia (2 Cor. 2.13). Indeed, it may be
that if he is using a genuine fragment in 1 Tim. 1.5 f it was
actually written by Paul at this time! It is improbable, of course,
that Luke would have been either capable of or interested in

unravelling Paul's dealings with the Corinthians in the way that modern scholars do. But the overall impression of the Corinthian letters would have been enough to show that his earlier narrative was incomplete, and it would have allowed considerable leeway for him to fit 1 Timothy into Paul's career.

The epistle to Titus offers the following information:

> This is why I left you in Crete, that you might amend what was defective, and appoint elders in every town as I directed you (1.5).

> When I send Artemas or Tychicus to you, do your best to come to me at Nicopolis, for I have decided to spend the winter there. Do your best to speed Zenas the lawyer and Apollos on their way; see that they lack nothing (3.12–13).

Titus is in Crete. Paul intends to winter in Nicopolis (of Epirus) and urges Titus to join him there. He plans to replace Titus with Artemas or Tychicus and urges him to take good care of Zenas and Apollos. Acts mentions neither Titus nor the evangelization of Crete. However, if we assume that Luke received this information after he had written Acts, we can still enquire whether he could have fitted it into his earlier outline of Paul's career. According to Acts, the only time Paul visited Crete was on his way to Rome (Acts 27.7 f), and this could scarcely be the setting for the epistle. Paul was a prisoner and the centurion in command was eager to reach Rome. Paul's stay in Corinth (Acts 18) is a possible setting, though less likely than the two-year stay in Ephesus (Acts 19).[2] More probable still is the setting afforded by Acts 20.3, during Paul's three-month stay in Greece. It is true that Acts 20.4 implies that Tychicus accompanied Paul to Jerusalem, but Luke could have assumed that Artemas rather than Tychicus relieved Titus (Tit. 3.12). The silence of Acts about Titus and the mission to Crete is strange, but not inexplicable. At the time he wrote Acts, Luke presumably did not know about them. The former he would have learned about from 2 Corinthians, and the latter presumably by word of mouth, for whoever wrote the epistle to Titus presumably had some tradition connecting Paul and Titus with Crete —even if it was an unreliable one. It is difficult to imagine that Crete would have been chosen arbitrarily as the fictitious setting when neither Acts nor the Pauline epistles allude to a mission there. When writing Titus, Luke could have fitted this new information easily into his earlier narrative. Indeed, he may have been using a genuine Pauline travel note (Tit. 3.12–15) and assumed it was connected with a mission in Crete when in reality it came from another context. P. N. Harrison, for example, suggests that it was written by Paul in W. Macedonia and sent to Titus in Corinth between the writing of 2 Cor. 10—13 and 2 Cor. 1—9. He then equates the trip of Paul into Macedonia in 2 Cor. 2.12 f; 7.5 f with Acts 20.1 f.[3]

The problems posed by 2 Timothy are more complex since it is far more informative about the circumstances and movements of Paul and his companions:

> You are aware that all who are in Asia turned away from me, and among them Phygelus and Hermogenes. May the Lord grant mercy to the household of Onesiphorus, for he often refreshed me; he was not ashamed of my chains, but when he arrived in Rome he searched for me eagerly and found me . . . (1.15–17).

> Now you have observed . . . my persecutions, my sufferings, what befell me at Antioch, at Iconium, and at Lystra, what persecutions I endured . . . (3.10–11).

> Do your best to come to me soon. For Demas, in love with this present world, has deserted me and gone to Thessalonica; Crescens has gone to Galatia. Titus to Dalmatia. Luke alone is with me. Get Mark and bring him with you, for he is very useful in serving me. Tychicus I have sent to Ephesus. When you come, bring the cloak I left with Carpus at Troas, also the books, and above all the parchments. Alexander the coppersmith did me great harm; the Lord will requite him for his deeds. Beware of him yourself, for he strongly opposed our message. At my first defence no one took my part; all deserted me. May it not be charged against them! But the Lord stood by me and gave me strength to proclaim the word fully, that all the Gentiles might hear it. So I was rescued from the lion's mouth. The Lord will rescue me from every evil and save me for his heavenly kingdom. To him be the glory for ever and ever. Amen. Greet Prisca and Aquila, and the household of Onesiphorus. Erastus remained at Corinth; Trophimus I left ill at Miletus. Do your best to come before winter. Eubulus sends greetings to you, as do Pudens and Linus and Claudia and all the brethren (4.9–21).

The major questions arising from these data are: how many imprisonments are referred to? Where does the author imagine Paul and Timothy to be when the epistle was written? Can the details be harmonized with the Pauline letters and, more importantly for our purposes, with Acts?

The first task is to consider whether 2 Timothy can be brought into line with Acts. Clearly, this would involve assuming that Acts 28 is the appropriate setting for 2 Timothy, since that is the only Roman captivity in Acts. And apart from 2 Tim. 1.17, which unambiguously refers to Rome as the place of Paul's captivity, the general impression given by 2 Timothy is that it is Paul's final epistle written immediately prior to his death (2 Tim. 4.6). On this interpretation the proclamation to 'all the Gentiles' (4.17) would refer to the witness Paul bore when on trial before the rulers of the pagan world, rather than to his release and subsequent missionary activity. The statement that despite Paul's incapacity, the preaching of the gospel continues unhindered (2 Tim. 2.9) accords well with the impression left by Acts 28.30–1. Similarly, Paul's freedom to confer and plan with his companions and their freedom to come and go (2 Tim. 4.9 f) fit the loose form of house arrest implied by Acts 28.30–1. Above all, this interpretation has the advantage of fitting 2 Timothy into what we know Luke knew of Paul's career when he wrote Acts—namely, that it ended in Rome. Although he does not describe Paul's death, Luke clearly states in Acts 20.17 f that Paul does not expect to see the Ephesian elders again (20.25, 58), since he can foresee only imprisonment and affliction ahead (Acts 20.23). The implication is that there was no further missionary work by Paul in Asia Minor and that he met his end in Rome (cf. Acts 21.10 f). Indeed, as we saw in the previous chapter, it may be that 2 Timothy confirms a recent explanation for the enigmatic ending of Acts, which tells neither of Paul's death nor of his release even though Luke presumably knew what had happened.[4]

There are, of course, objections to the equation of Acts 28 and 2 Timothy:

1 First, in 2 Tim. 4.13 Paul asks Timothy to 'bring the cloak which I left with Carpus at Troas, also the books, and above all the parchments'. According to Acts, Paul's last visit to Troas was on his way to Jerusalem (Acts 20.6–13), so that there was an

interval of at least three years, and more if 2 Timothy is located towards the end of the two-year Roman captivity, before Paul decided to collect his belongings. It is difficult, though not impossible, to assume that Luke could have imagined this to be the case.

2   According to Acts 20.4 f Timothy was one of Paul's companions on his trip to Jerusalem and Rome. However, as we noted earlier, given the vagueness of Luke's chronological data in Acts, it is not difficult to suppose that at a later date he assumed that Timothy had either stayed in Troas (Acts 20.5) and later moved down to Ephesus (2 Tim. 4.12 probably implies that the author thought Timothy was in Ephesus), or that he had stayed behind with the Ephesian elders (Acts 20.35 f), or that he had returned to Ephesus during Paul's imprisonment in Caesarea (Acts 24.27).

3   According to 2 Tim. 4.20 Paul 'left Trophimus ill in Miletus'. Yet in Acts 20.4 he is listed as one of Paul's companions and in Acts 21.29 appears in Jerusalem with Paul. Moreover, Paul's final visit to Miletus in Acts is described in Acts 20.15–37. If Luke assumed that Trophimus' illness and recovery took place between Acts 20.37 and 21.29, it is difficult to imagine why Paul should tell Timothy about it three or more years later, especially when Timothy was in nearby Ephesus! There have been various attempts to explain this: *apelipon* (2 Tim. 4.20) could be read as third person ('he, i.e. Erastus, left Trophimus sick . . .') rather than first person; or one could emend *Meleto* (Miletus) to *Melite* (Malta) and see it as a reference to the events described in Acts 28.1 f.[5] Maybe as a result of receiving new information Luke assumed there was a visit to Miletus on the way to Rome, or realized that the reference to Trophimus in Jerusalem (Acts 21.29) was a mistake. Perhaps more probable than any of these ingenious suggestions is the view that Luke simply did not notice the discrepancy between 2 Tim. 4.20 and his earlier narrative. It is not difficult to suppose that the author of Acts, which is full of discrepancies and lacunae, would continue this trend in later writings, especially if there was a gap of a few years between writing 2 Timothy and Acts and he did not have the latter in front of him when he wrote the former. This would be all the more likely if Luke was using a genuine Pauline travel note in 2 Tim. 4.9 f.

Indeed, this may finally be the simplest explanation of 2 Tim. 4.9 f—that it is a genuine travel note, written by Paul from Caesarea, which Luke misplaces in Rome. The correspondence between 2 Tim. 4.9 f and the circumstances surrounding Paul's Caesarean captivity is remarkable.[6] Caesarea would be a natural centre for journeys to Dalmatia, Thessalonica, Ephesus, and Galatia (2 Tim. 4.10, 12). On his way to Caesarea Paul stopped in Troas (Acts 20.5; 2 Tim. 4.13), Miletus (Acts 20.15 f; 2 Tim. 4.20), and probably in Corinth (Acts 20.3; 2 Tim. 4.20; cf. 2 Cor. 12.13; 14.1). The reference to the cloak, books, and parchments (2 Tim. 4.13) can be connected with the journey on foot to Assos (Acts 20.13) soon after Passover (Acts 20.6), for with the beginning of the warm weather Paul would not have needed his cloak until the following winter in Caesarea. 2 Tim. 4.16–18 could be connected with Paul's defence either before the Sanhedrin (Acts 23.1–11, cf. esp. Acts 23.11; 2 Tim. 4.17), Felix (Acts 24.1 f), or Festus (Acts 25.6 f). Acts does not mention the desertion of Paul by his friends in Caesarea (2 Tim. 4.9–12, 16) but it is not inconceivable that this occurred. The conditions of his imprisonment, according to Acts 24.23, would have allowed the comings and goings of 2 Tim. 4.9–22. Whichever of the various hearings is identified with the 'first defence' of 2 Tim. 4.16, none of them was conclusive and could have led to the statement in 2 Tim. 4.17, either as a reference to witness during a Roman trial or as an expectation of release and further missionary endeavour. The only objections to supposing that 2 Tim. 4.9–22 is a genuine fragment written by Paul from Caesarea arise in the narrative of Acts, in particular the movements of Timothy and Trophimus. Perhaps with regard to Timothy's movements Acts is vague and incomplete (as in 19.22; 20.5), and with regard to Trophimus' movements simply wrong. Or maybe there is something to be said for the view that 2 Tim. 4.9–18 was written from Caesarea and 4.19–22 from elsewhere and that Luke has mistakenly conflated these two genuine fragments. Certainly the problem of Trophimus' movements is not sufficient reason to reject the overwhelming evidence in favour of the Caesarean origin of 2 Tim. 4.9 f. Luke mistakenly assigns it to Paul's Roman captivity, using it as the peg on which to hang the rest of 2 Timothy.

4   There is one other possible objection to the thesis that Luke

thought that 2 Timothy was written during the Roman captivity
of Acts 28. It could be argued that the description of Paul's
situation in 2 Tim. 4 does not concur with that given in the
captivity epistles (Colossians, Philippians, Philemon) which are
traditionally set in Rome. There Paul is surrounded by many of his
friends: Timothy (Col. 1.1; Phil. 1.1; Philem. 1), Demas (Col.
4.14; Philem. 24), Mark (Col. 4.10; Philem. 24), Epaphras (Col.
4.12; Philem. 23), Aristarchus (Col. 4.10; Philem. 24), Luke (Col.
4.14; Philem. 24) and Jesus Justus (Col. 4.11). Of these the first
three, according to 2 Tim. 4.9 f, had left Paul; indeed, the only
point of agreement is that Luke was with Paul. With respect to our
thesis of the Lucan authorship of the Pastorals, however, this is not
a serious objection. It is possible that Luke did not know these
later epistles of Paul and would thus have been unaware of any
conflict. Maybe he knew that Paul had written letters from Rome,
but had not seen them, and this in part inspired the setting for 2
Timothy. On the other hand, if he knew the captivity epistles
perhaps he knew that they had been sent from Caesarea and not
from Rome. Or, if they were in fact sent from Rome, maybe he
mistakenly believed that they were sent from Caesarea. This would
then have been good reason for him to place the fragment (2 Tim.
4.9–22) in Rome, since it conflicted with the information in the
captivity epistles! On the assumption that Luke knew the captivity
epistles, however, a simpler explanation would suffice. Luke knew
that Paul's Roman captivity was lengthy and relatively un-
restricted, and he could have assumed that the captivity epistles
reflected the earlier period of that imprisonment when Paul was
still hoping for release (Phil. 1.25; Philem. 22) and was surrounded
by his friends, and that 2 Tim. 4.9 f reflected the situation during
the final few months, when his friends had left and martyrdom was
imminent.

So far we have considered the setting of the Pastorals in relation to
the narrative in Acts. There is a quite different, and simpler, way
of arguing that Luke wrote the Pastorals, and that is to revive the
theory that Paul was imprisoned in Rome on two occasions. It has
often been argued that 2 Timothy presupposes such a view. Thus
2 Tim. 1.16–18 is taken to refer to the first captivity, which is the
same as that described in Acts 28. The phrase 'during my first
trial (*apologia*)' in 2 Tim. 4.16 may also imply two trials, though it

could also refer to the first of two hearings during the same trial (the Roman *prima actio*). 2 Tim. 1.8, 12; 2.9; 4.6–12, 16–19, 21 would then refer to the second captivity in Rome, while the information in 2 Tim. 1.15, 18; 3.11; 4.14 could refer to activity either before the first imprisonment or during the interim between the two. 2 Tim. 4.13, 17, 20 would also be assigned to this interim period.

This view would clearly be as advantageous to our hypothesis as it would to the defence of Pauline authorship. The supposition would be that after the captivity described in Acts 28 Paul was released and travelled again to the east, visiting his old haunts. During this period he wrote 1 Timothy and Titus. During his second and final imprisonment he wrote 2 Timothy. In this way all the personalia and chronological details of the Pastorals which appear to contradict Acts or the Pauline epistles are swept into the period beyond Acts 28. Luke would have had no problem in locating the Pastorals in Paul's career, since they are assigned to a period during which he produced no other writings and which take up where the narrative of Acts leaves off.

This interpretation of Paul's career goes back as far as Eusebius and was accepted by others such as Jerome and Chrysostom.[7] In addition, it is argued, there are several allusions to Paul's travels after his first trip to Rome. In Rom. 15.24, 28 Paul expresses his intention to go to Spain after visiting Rome. The Acts of Peter and the Muratorian Canon (lines 34–9) clearly imply that Paul fulfilled this intention.[8] Clement of Rome (writing *c*. A.D. 96), in a notoriously obscure passage, provides information that might imply the same (1 Clem. 5.7). And if Philippians and Philemon were written from Rome, it is significant that in them Paul announces that he hopes to be released, though in these letters he plans to travel to the east rather than the west. Moreover, it could be argued that if Luke knew that Paul had been released after his first Roman captivity and continued his work, the abrupt ending of Acts is more understandable than if he knew Paul was put to death. It might be said that if he had narrated Paul's release it would have provided a triumphant conclusion to his story and would have vindicated once and for all Roman justice. But it is not clear how important the theme of Roman justice was to Luke and it is at least arguable that the narrative of Acts is more concerned with the progress of the gospel in the Gentile world than it is with the career of Paul. On this view Acts 28.30–1 *is* a triumphant conclusion to the preceding narrative. Finally, it has been suggested that in Roman law if a man's accusers failed to put their case within a statutory two-year period, the charge was automatically dropped. Thus, it is said, Acts 28.30–1 actually implies that Paul was released.[9]

We might conclude, therefore, that all the available evidence about Paul's later career either points to or is consistent with the theory of a second Roman imprisonment. There are, however, many difficulties. First, the evidence for Paul's release is questionable: Philippians and Philemon may express an expectation which was not fulfilled; K. Lake's interpretation of Acts 28 is dubious;[10] 1 Clem. 5.7 is ambiguous and may not refer to a journey to Spain. Moreover, Eusebius is not an independent witness since he merely interprets the data in 2 Timothy, and the references in the Acts of Peter and the Muratorian Canon may be no more than legendary glosses on Rom. 15. Second, even if one accepts the argument in favour of a second imprisonment, there is a discrepancy between the Pastorals which refer only to activity east of Rome, and much of the other evidence, which refers only to travels west of Rome. Moreover, Acts 20.25, 38 clearly imply that when Luke wrote Acts he believed that Paul would not be in Asia Minor again. Third, all the data in 2 Timothy are consistent with the view that there was only one Roman imprisonment. 2 Tim. 1.17 and 4.16–18 could refer to the same captivity, and 2 Timothy itself could be set in the period after Paul's successful first hearing (2 Tim. 4.16) and prior to his imminent and fateful second hearing.

Before we conclude we must consider the reference in 2 Tim. 3.11 to Timothy's observation of Paul's suffering at Antioch, Iconium, and Lystra. If this is an allusion to Acts 13—14 it might be taken to militate against Lucan authorship, since according to Acts Timothy becomes Paul's companion only after the Apostolic Council (Acts 16.1 f). It is possible that 2 Tim. 3.11 reflects traditions about (and perhaps emanating from) Timothy which came to Luke after he had written Acts. However, it should be noted that there is no essential contradiction here. According to Acts 16.1–2 Timothy was already a believer and was well known in Lystra and Iconium before he met Paul. Thus while he may not have been Paul's companion during his first missionary journey he would have been well-informed of his activities. The verb 'follow' (*parakoloutheo*) is thus used loosely—or perhaps it means 'take as an example' rather than 'follow' in a physical sense (cf. 1 Cor. 4.17).[11]

We have now surveyed all the chronological and personal data in the Pastorals. If in defence of our hypothesis it is thought necessary to show that the setting and details of the Pastorals must conform to Luke's earlier account of his career, then two replies are possible. If Paul was released from his first Roman imprisonment and Luke knew this, then he would have had no difficulty in locating the Pastorals in Paul's subsequent career. The arguments for this are, however, questionable. It is a possible, though not a probable, solution. If Luke had had to locate the Pastorals in Acts he would have had no problems with 1 Timothy and Titus. 2 Timothy, set in Rome, creates a few discrepancies with his earlier account, but none of them serious and none of them any greater than the discrepancies between the Gospel and Acts or within Acts itself! Yet after this exhaustive tour of the evidence, it is quite conceivable that we are barking up the wrong tree. If Luke wrote the Pastorals some years after he had written Acts, to counter the influence of false teachers, the pressure of the immediate situation was probably such that he would not have been at all concerned to fit them precisely into his earlier narrative of Paul's career. This would have been so particularly if he based the Pastorals on some genuine fragments of Pauline correspondence and if he did not have a copy of Acts in front of him when he wrote. In these circumstances the problem of locating 1 Timothy and Titus at a precise point in his earlier narrative may not have arisen, and 2 Timothy may simply have been assigned in a rather loose fashion to the period of Paul's imprisonment in Rome.

11
Conclusion

The evidence we have discussed can be summarized as follows: first, there is a large number of linguistic and stylistic similarities between Luke–Acts and the Pastorals which, in view of the brevity of the Pastorals and the change of genre, are remarkable. Second, in their approach to many themes Luke–Acts and the Pastorals reveal a similar, and often identical, stance. And this is not simply a matter of common ideas and language but, as we saw especially in the chapter on christology, also of an identical technique in compilation. Third, where there are differences they are differences of emphasis, and they are readily explicable when one bears in mind the difference in genre, subject-matter, and *Sitz im Leben* between Luke–Acts and the Pastorals. Fourth, an analysis of the data often reveals the weakness of the hypothesis of Pauline authorship of the Pastorals. In those areas where the Pastorals most clearly diverge from Paul, they agree most closely with Luke–Acts. Certainly, given a choice between Paul and Luke as the author of the Pastorals, Luke is a far more likely candidate.

This evidence could be explained in a number of ways. First, it has been argued that the similarities between Luke and the Pastor are coincidental, the result of both authors reflecting the general milieu of Pauline Christianity in the generation after Paul. Within this broad view there are various specific ways of explaining the similarities between Luke and the Pastor, and these we considered in our discussion of the relationship between Acts 20.17 f and 2 Timothy.[1] This is not, in my view, an adequate explanation since I believe that the similarities between Luke and the Pastor are far more extensive than the protagonists of this view have recognized. N. Brox, for example, having undercut and dismissed some of A. Strobel's arguments, thinks that what remains does not provide strong enough evidence for joint authorship. But while he has correctly rejected some of Strobel's evidence,[2] there is much that remains and, as I have tried to show, the evidence is at any rate far more extensive than Strobel indicated. One can, of course, point to other documents which have affinities with Luke–Acts and the Pastorals. Luke–Acts share a number of terms with Hebrews,[3] while the Pastorals have affinities with 2 Peter[4] and Polycarp.[5] The similarities are, in these cases, to be explained by a common milieu or perhaps, in the case of Polycarp, by the dependence of one writer (Polycarp) on another (Pastor). But with these documents one is concerned at the most with only a few similarities, whereas the argument for common authorship of the Pastorals and Luke–Acts is based on an extensive accumulation of evidence. And the evidence must be allowed its cumulative force, for while one strand alone may not take the strain of this hypothesis, the combination of several strands may.

A second option is to think in terms of a Lucan school or circle, in which the author of Luke–Acts would be thought of as the leading light and one of his disciples, influenced by Lucan language and perspectives, as the author of the Pastorals. This would allow one to take account of the similarities between Luke–Acts and the Pastorals without going so far as to propose common authorship. An analogy with the school of Matthew[6] and the Johannine school[7] is, of course, what is in mind. Whether, strictly speaking, one can refer to a Lucan 'school' rather than the vaguer notion of a Lucan circle of influence or group of churches is a matter of little concern for our hypothesis. The relationship between such a Lucan school and the Pauline school, if the latter existed, is a matter of conjecture. H. Conzelmann[8] thinks there was a Pauline school (probably in Ephesus) but that Luke deliberately stood apart from it despite much common ground. There may be truth in this and, as long as Luke is allowed to take the Pastorals with him, it would serve our purpose as well. On the other hand, it may be possible to speak of a Lucan wing within a broader school, bearing in mind the differences, for example, between Colossians/Ephesians and Luke and the Pastorals. Perhaps Polycarp, too, was part of this Lucan school. The Johannine school offers adequate proof that there could be a variety in both literary genre and viewpoint within the same circles. This, it would seem to me, is an improvement on the first explanation we considered and a viable option. But it does not go far enough. The combination of linguistic, theological, and historical parallels seems to me to point beyond the notion of influence to that of common authorship, and this is our third option.

The argument for Lucan authorship of the Pastorals can be pursued on different levels. C. F. D. Moule, as we have seen, argues for a combination of Lucan and Pauline influence. Luke wrote the letters, but under the direction of Paul. He was more than a mere amanuensis, however, since he was allowed considerable freedom to use his own language and style and his own version of Paul's teaching. This, Moule supposes, was because Paul did not dictate the letters but simply outlined the gist of what he wanted to say and left Luke to say it for him. The Pastorals, therefore, were written before Acts (and probably before the Gospel), during the interim between Paul's first and second Roman captivities. A. Strobel, though he is not too clear on the matter, appears to hold a similar view.[9]

This is not an impossible explanation of the data we have discussed, but there are objections that can be raised. For example, the Pastorals indicate a situation where both church order and gnostic influence were more advanced and developed than they are in Acts. Now one could argue that Acts, although written after the Pastorals, is an accurate record of an earlier era and does not in any substantial way reflect the situation of the author's day. If, however, as we have argued, this is not so, it would suggest that Acts was written before the Pastorals. Moule's dependence on the second imprisonment theory is a further weakness, since it is a possible, though not probable, explanation of the evidence. Moreover, on Moule's view two omissions from Acts are difficult to explain: first, the failure to mention that Paul was released from the imprisonment in Acts 28; and second, the absence of any reference to Paul's correspondence with his aides and the communities he had founded. It seems, therefore, that if one is to argue for common authorship, the view that the Pastorals were written after Acts and for a different purpose is more satisfactory.

How did Luke come to write the Pastorals? Here we have to use our imagination and the best place to begin is to consider how he came to possess the material used in the composition of Acts. E. Haenchen suggests various possibilities.[10] Perhaps Luke travelled to some of the important Pauline communities and questioned the older members who could remember sufficiently far back. Also, he might have asked friends and acquaintances to glean as much information as they could on their travels. Or he may have written to the communities and asked them to send information. This search for material, Haenchen notes, would have been no easy task, any more than collecting the material for his Gospel would have been (cf. Luke 4.1–4). It would have required a determined and persistent individual who placed high value on the task. When he had gathered enough material he wrote Acts—using anecdotes, recollections, and possibly some longer written sources such as a travel diary or an Antiochene source (though Haenchen doubts this). Part of the motive in writing Acts was to defend Paul and the Pauline communities from Jewish and Jewish–Christian attacks.

Luke, therefore, would have become known as the man who collected information about the development of early Christianity and presumably, after he had completed Acts, new material continued to come his way. It could have come in various forms: oral tradition about the life and teaching of Paul; copies of some of Paul's letters in their original form; and fragments of correspondence Paul had written to friends and acquaintances describing his whereabouts and proposed movements. It may even be that he had heard that Paul corresponded with Timothy and Titus, believed the fragments he possessed were part of that correspondence, and so composed the Pastoral letters giving to the best of his ability what he thought Paul would have written. The immediate cause of composition, however, was not merely an antiquarian interest in reconstructing Paul's correspondence, but an urgent and pressing problem. False teachers were becoming increasingly influential, teaching a form of gnosticism whose speculation was based on the Old Testament and, more distressing still, whose ostensible authority was Paul himself. To counter this Luke wrote three epistles in the name of Paul giving what he imagined Paul's response would have been under the circumstances.

A different approach would be to suppose that the Pastorals were the planned 'third volume' of a trilogy, Luke–Acts making up the first two volumes.[11] This would allow one to explain some of the differences between Acts and the Pastorals by supposing that certain things are omitted in Acts because Luke planned to mention them in the Pastorals. Thus the ending of Acts might be uninformative because further details were planned for 2 Timothy.

This could be combined with the view that there were significant
changes during the interim between Acts and the Pastorals by
arguing that while the Pastorals were planned well in advance, the
change of circumstances after the completion of Acts meant that
the 'third volume' did not turn out quite as planned. But that the
situation did change in the way I have suggested seems to me to be
essential to the argument for common authorship, whatever form
it takes.

Many things, of course, remain unclear. The date of the
Pastorals, like that of Acts, can never certainly be established. I
would guess at 85–90 A.D. for Acts and 90–95 for the Pastorals, but
it is little more than a guess. That Luke–Acts and the Pastorals
were written for the same communities need not be assumed.
Perhaps it was not the case that the same groups were plagued at
one stage by anti-Pauline polemic from Jews or Jewish Christians
and later by pro-Pauline Jewish gnostics. That Christian communities in the same geographical area could have different
problems seems to be indicated in the Book of Revelation. In the
letters to the seven churches in Asia Minor, two communities are
warned about Jewish opponents (Rev. 2.9; 3.9) while others seem
to be troubled by gnostic Nicolaitans (Rev. 2.6, 15).[12] On the other
hand, the Gospel and Epistles of John offer an interesting parallel
to the suggestion that the same group could be faced with both
problems, for it is widely agreed that these works come from the
same milieu. When the epistles were written the disputes between
Church and synagogue evident in the Gospel had either dis-
appeared or become less significant, and the problem of false
teachers of a gnostic–docetic type had become the major issue.
This would indicate that there was a similar change of circumstances to that which took place between the writing of Acts and
the Pastorals.

Assuming that Acts and the Pastorals were addressed to the same
group of churches, we still cannot locate them with any certainty.
Asia Minor is commonly taken to be the milieu of Luke–Acts and
the Pastorals, and this is probably correct. There is something to
be said, however, for Rome as the place of composition for Luke–
Acts (and the Pastorals). The climax in Rome (Acts 28, cf. Acts
1.8; 2 Tim.) might suggest this as well as 'the image of the
Imperium and the reduction of the geographical horizon to the
orbis Romanus'.[13] It has recently been suggested that the list of

nations[14] in Acts 2.9–11 and the 'we' passages in Acts[15] are written from a Roman perspective. There are interesting connections with 1 Clement: traditions about Peter and Paul (1 Clem. 5) and the other apostles (1 Clem. 42); the 'third generation' perspective and the concept of church order, which Luke and 1 Clement share with the Pastorals. The connection between the christology of Luke–Acts and the Pastorals and the 'Roman' confession of faith, the early form of the Apostolic creed, has also been noted.[16] There are problems, of course, not the least of which is Luke's ignorance of Romans and 1 Corinthians. 1 Clement, for example, knows the latter, yet apparently does not know any of the canonical Gospels. Perhaps all we can say is that there is a certain 'Roman' perspective in Acts which may be because the author lived in Rome, because he had once lived in Rome but now lived elsewhere (Asia Minor?), or perhaps simply because some of the traditions and sources he used were written from a Roman perspective. The Pastorals do not help us a great deal, since they give so few indications of their place of composition that they could be located almost anywhere.

A similar vagueness is inevitable when we consider the possibility that Luke was involved in the collection of the *Corpus Paulinum*. E. J. Goodspeed believes that the publication of Acts inspired the search for and publication of Paul's letters.[17] But since Luke never refers to Paul writing letters this is implausible. C. F. D. Moule suggests that Luke may have been the collector of Paul's writings.[18] This would concur with our view that Luke, after the publication of Acts, continued to search for and receive information about Paul. That he knew some Pauline letters when he wrote the Pastorals seems plausible. That he knew them all is possible, but not likely. Maybe we might assume that he completed the collection of the *Corpus Paulinum* after he wrote the Pastorals. But in view of the absence of any evidence, we can do no more than propose him as a likely candidate for this role.

In conclusion, it is perhaps useful to reflect on some of the implications of the view that Luke wrote the Pastorals. First, it provides us with an oblique approach to the question of Pauline authorship of the Pastorals. The close parallels with Luke and the differences from Paul show that a far stronger case can be made for Lucan than for Pauline authorship. Second, we are given a new vantage-point from which to assess the complex problems of Luke–Acts. This is to some extent, of course, a circular argument, since the case for Lucan authorship of the Pastorals is dependent to no small degree on one's interpretation of Luke–Acts. We must, however, bear two things in mind. First, there is considerable agreement among scholars in their interpretation of the Pastorals — to about the same extent as there is disagreement in their interpretation of Acts. Second, there is a remarkable affinity between Luke–Acts and the Pastorals which it would be difficult to contest even if one was not persuaded by the case for common authorship. Thus the evidence we have considered sheds some light on the problems of Luke–Acts, in particular on the type of writer and thinker Luke was and how he used the sources and traditions available to him in the composition of his work. There are those who view Luke as an independent and original thinker, a theologian with a consistent point of view and an artist who has complete mastery and control over his materials. The connection between Luke–Acts and the Pastorals, however, shows him in a different light. Here he creates the impression of being more of an eclectic, one who willingly uses diverse traditions and who is more concerned to preserve and transmit information than to interpret it or weave it into an overall design. Both of these conceptions are consistent with the view that Luke was concerned with the problems of the Church of his day, but the latter would portray him as more pragmatic and conservative, less sophisticated and original, than the former. The distinction should not perhaps be drawn too firmly. The mere shift from narrative to epistle undoubtedly helps to create a different impression. Moreover, it may well be that in Luke–Acts the author provides evidence both for careful design in his use of literary patterns and for a certain imprecision on theological matters, whereas the latter trait would naturally be more evident in the composition of the Pastorals. The least that must be conceded, however, is that there is more than one facet to the Lucan mind.

To argue that Luke wrote the Pastorals is implicitly to challenge those who, on the basis of the portrait of Paul in general or the office of apostle in particular, assign Luke–Acts and the Pastorals to quite different streams of post-apostolic Christianity.[19] In the chapter on the portrait of Paul we argued that the same man could have been responsible for both. The failure of the Pastorals to mention apostles other than Paul was not the result of ignorance or antipathy, but simply because it was irrelevant to the circumstances in which they were written. This suggests that if an early Christian writer ignores traditions about Paul or the other apostles, one should not jump to the conclusion that he intends to slight them. Undoubtedly the silence is on occasions deliberate, but unless there are indications to this effect, other explanations should not be excluded. The classification of early Christian writers will otherwise become both unnecessarily rigid and also misleading.

Finally, if Luke wrote the Pastorals in addition to Luke–Acts, he stands as one of the most important figures in the New Testament, not only because of the sheer volume of his writings, but also because of his dominant role as an interpreter of first-century Christianity and a defender of the Church in its disputes with Jewish and gnostic opponents. And even if one reduces the argument and thinks in terms of a Lucan school, this would scarcely diminish his role.

Notes

CHAPTER 1 INTRODUCTION

1   S. G. Wilson, *The Gentiles and the Gentile Mission in Luke–Acts* (Cambridge 1973).

2   A. T. Hanson, *The Pastoral Letters* (Cambridge 1966), p. 15.

3   C. F. D. Moule, 'The Problem of the Pastoral Epistles: A Reappraisal', *BJRL*, 47 (1965), 430–52, quotation 434. See also *The Birth of the New Testament* (London 1966), pp. 220–1.

4   A. Strobel, 'Schreiben des Lukas? Zum sprachlichen Problem der Pastoralbriefe', *NTS*, 15 (1969), 191–210.

5   Strobel, 'Schreiben', 204–5.

6   N. Brox, 'Lukas als Verfasser der Pastoralbriefe?' *JAC*, 13 (1970), 62–77.

7   Brox, 'Lukas', 72 f.

8   P. N. Harrison, *The Problem of the Pastoral Epistles* (London 1921), p. 88.

9   H. Gamble, 'The Redaction of the Pauline Letters and the Formation of the Pauline Corpus', *JBL*, 94 (1975), 403–18, here 417 n. 36.

10   Harrison, *Problem*, pp. 87 f.

CHAPTER 2 LANGUAGE AND STYLE

1   Strobel, 'Schreiben', 194–201; Moule, 'Problem', 439 f; C. Spicq, *Les Épîtres pastorales* (4th edn, Paris 1969), pp. 233–9.

2   These and the following lists are, with minor modifications, those of Strobel.

3   A. Plummer, *The Gospel According to St Luke* (Edinburgh 1910), p. 330.

4   Strobel, 'Schreiben', 199.

5   Harrison, *Problem*, p. 53.

6   Strobel, 'Schreiben', 200.

7   Strobel, 'Schreiben', 200–1.

8 Strobel, 'Schreiben', 201.

9 A. W. Argyle, 'The Greek of Luke and Acts', *NTS*, 20 (1974), 441–5.

CHAPTER 3 ESCHATOLOGY

1 Wilson, *Gentiles*, pp. 59–87. The seminal works were H. Conzelmann, *The Theology of St Luke* (London 1960), and E. Lohse, 'Lukas als Theologie der Heilsgeschichte', *Ev. Th.*, 14 (1954), 256 f.

2 R. Hiers, 'The Problem of the Delay of the Parousia in Luke–Acts', *NTS*, 20 (1974), 145–55, quotation 146.

3 E. Franklin, *Christ the Lord: A Study in the Purpose and Theology of Luke–Acts* (Philadelphia 1975), pp. 9–47, quotation p. 28.

4 Wilson, *Gentiles*, p. 28.

5 R. Bultmann, *Theology of the New Testament* (London 1955), vol ii, p. 185. For Luke, see E. Earle Ellis, 'Present and Future Eschatology in Luke', *NTS*, 12 (1965–6), 27–41.

6 E. F. Scott, *The Pastoral Epistles* (London 1936), p. 118. Cf. pp. xxxiii, 78–9, 169. Also J. N. D. Kelly, *A Commentary on the Pastoral Epistles* (London 1963), pp. 94, 145, 193, 246; B. S. Easton, *The Pastoral Epistles* (Philadelphia 1972), pp. 10, 89, 104.

7 Bultmann, *Theology*, vol. ii, p. 185. See also M. Dibelius and H. Conzelmann, *The Pastoral Epistles* (Philadelphia 1972), pp. 27, 62, 139; Hanson, *Pastoral*, p. 91.

8 W. Bauer, *A Greek-English Lexicon of the New Testament and other Early Christian Literature* revised and adapted by W. F. Arndt and F. W. Gingrich (Chicago 1957), p. 857. Cf. C. K. Barrett, *The Pastoral Epistles* (Oxford 1963), p. 67; Kelly, *Pastoral*, p. 94; Hanson, *Pastoral*, p. 48.

9 H. G. Liddell and R. Scott, *A Greek-English Lexicon* (8th edn, Oxford 1897), p. 1647, give no examples of the superlative meaning; and Bauer admits it may be comparative.

10 So Easton, *Pastoral*, pp. 138–9.

11 Dibelius-Conzelmann, *Pastoral*, p. 64; N. Brox, *Die Pastoralbriefe* (Regensburg 1969), pp. 166–7.

12 Dibelius-Conzelmann, *Pastoral*, p. 10.

13 E. Haenchen, *The Acts of the Apostles* (Oxford 1971), p. 179.

14 Kelly, *Pastoral*, p. 145.

15 S. Schulz, 'Gottes Vorsehung bei Lk.', *ZNW*, 54 (1963), 104 f.

16 Bultmann, *Theology*, vol. ii, p. 185; Dibelius-Conzelmann, *Pastoral*, pp. 10, 89, 104.

17 Kelly, *Pastoral*, p. 246. Cf. D. Guthrie, *The Pastoral Epistles* (London 1957), p. 199.

18 Wilson, *Gentiles*, pp. 59–87. See also the balanced discussion in C. Burchard, *Der dreizehnte Zeuge* (Göttingen 1970), pp. 176–83.

19 Dibelius-Conzelmann, *Pastoral*, p. 89.

CHAPTER 4 SALVATION

1 Cf. especially W. Foerster, G. Fohrer, art. *sozo*, *TDNT*, vii, pp. 965–1024; I. Howard Marshall, *Luke, Historian and Theologian* (Exeter 1970), pp. 77 f.

2 Foerster, *TDNT*, vii, pp. 992–3.

3 *Contra*, Foerster, *TDNT*, vii, p. 997.

4 Conzelmann, *Luke*, pp. 199–201; U. Wilckens, *Die Missionsreden in der Apostelgeschichte* (3rd edn, Neukirchen 1974), pp. 77, 184–5, 216–17; Wilson, *Gentiles*, pp. 49–50.

5 For a discussion see Marshall, *Luke*, pp. 173–4.

6 Marshall, *Luke*, p. 174.

7 Kelly, *Pastoral*, p. 18.

8 Dibelius-Conzelmann, *Pastoral*, pp. 41–2; Scott, *Pastoral*, p. 22; Kelly, *Pastoral*, p. 64, calls it a 'theological cliché'.

9 Barrett, *Pastoral*, p. 138. See pp. 31–2 below.

10 Barrett, *Pastoral*, p. 141.

11 Dibelius-Conzelmann, *Pastoral*, p. 150.

12 Haenchen, *Acts*, p. 412. Cf. H. Conzelmann, *Die Apostelgeschichte* (Tübingen 1963), p. 77. *Contra* P. Vielhauer, 'On the "Paulinism" of Acts', *Studies in Luke–Acts*, ed. L. E. Keck and J. L. Martyn (London 1968), p. 42. This book is hereinafter designated as *SLA*.

13 H. Conzelmann, art. *charis*, *TDNT*, ix, pp. 372–402.

14 Conzelmann, *TDNT*, ix, p. 393, argues persuasively for a different translation.

15 Cf. Dibelius-Conzelmann, *Pastoral*, pp. 28–9; G. W. Knight, III, *The Faithful Sayings in the Pastoral Epistles* (Kampen 1968). He suggests that Luke may have been the collector of the faithful sayings and Paul's amanuensis (pp. 150–2).

16 Bultmann, art. *pisteuein*, *TDNT*, vi, pp. 174–228, here p. 219.

17 Wilson, *Gentiles*, p. 171 f.

18 Wilson, *Gentiles*, pp. 217–18.

19 Marshall, *Luke*, p. 190.

20 See commentaries ad loc.

21 Barrett, *Pastoral*, p. 92; Kelly, *Pastoral*, p. 156.

22 *Contra* Dibelius-Conzelmann, *Pastoral*, p. 98; Brox, *Pastoralbriefe*, p. 227.

CHAPTER 5 THE CHRISTIAN CITIZEN

1 Conzelmann, *Theology*, pp. 139–41; H. J. Cadbury, *The Making of Luke–Acts* (London 1961), p. 309.

2 Conzelmann, *Theology*, pp. 138–44, quotation p. 142.

3 C. K. Barrett, *Luke the Historian in Recent Study* (London 1961), p. 63.

4 J. C. O'Neill, *The Theology of Acts in its Historical Setting* (London 1961), pp. 166 f.

5 P. W. Walasky, 'The Trial and death of Jesus in the Gospel of Luke', *JBL*, 94 (1975), 81–93, here 85.

6 Conzelmann, *Theology*, p. 138.

7 C. E. B. Cranfield, 'The Christian's Political Responsibility', *SJT*, 15 (1962), 176–92.

8 G. Delling, art. *hupotassesthai*, *TDNT*, viii, p. 45.

9 Barrett, *Pastoral*, p. 139; also in *New Testament Essays* (London 1972), pp. 15–16.

10 J. T. Sanders, *Ethics in the New Testament* (Philadelphia 1975), p. 88. The quotation refers to 2 Thessalonians and 1 Peter as well as the Pastorals.

11 Dibelius-Conzelmann, *Pastoral*, p. 40.

12 Barrett, *Pastoral*, p. 50.

13 Barrett, *Essays*, p. 17.

14 E. Stauffer, *New Testament Theology* (London 1963), pp. 349–51; C. H. Dodd, *The Epistle of Paul to the Romans* (London 1959), pp. 208–11; A. Nygren, *Commentary on Romans* (Philadelphia 1972), pp. 427–31.

15 *Contra* J. Héring, *A Good and a Bad Government* (Illinois 1954), pp. 15–16.

16 *Contra* E. Käsemann, *New Testament Questions of Today* (London 1969), pp. 213 f.

17 O. Michel, *Der Brief an die Römer* (Göttingen 1966), p. 314.

18 Dodd, *Romans*, p. 210.

19 Nygren, *Romans*, p. 429, has a similar view.

20 So, for example, Barrett, *Essays*, pp. 15–16.

21 This concept of sin is, of course, found elsewhere in the New Testament. Cf. G. Stahlin, art. *hamartano*, *TDNT*, i, pp. 295–6.

22 J. L. Houlden, *Ethics and the New Testament* (London 1973), p. 64.

23 Houlden, *Ethics*, p. 56.

24 Conzelmann, *Theology*, pp. 231–2.

25 For the following paragraph see particularly Moule, 'Problem', 443–4. Cf. also Marshall, *Luke*, pp. 142–3, 206–8.

26 *Contra* Sanders, *Ethics*, p. 35.

27 Bultmann, *Theology*, vol. ii, p. 184. See further W. Foerster, art. *eusebes*, *TDNT*, vii, pp. 175 f.

28 *Contra* Foerster, art. cit., p. 181.

29 Cf. U. Luck, art. *sophron*, *TDNT*, viii, pp. 1097–104, here p. 1102.

30 Dibelius-Conzelmann, *Pastoral*, p. 20. *Contra* C. Maurer, art. *sunoida*, *TDNT*, vii, pp. 899–919, here p. 918.

CHAPTER 6 CHURCH AND MINISTRY

1 Strobel, 'Schreiben', 207.

2 So, for example, Barrett, *Pastoral*, p. 72; Kelly, *Pastoral*, p. 106; D. Daube, *The New Testament and Rabbinic Judaism* (London 1956), pp. 224–46; J. Jeremias, '*Presbuterion* ausserchristlich bezeugt', *ZNW*, 48 (1957), 127–32.

3 The arguments are those of G. Bornkamm, art. *presbuteros*, *TDNT*, vi, p. 666 n. 92. Cf. Dibelius-Conzelmann, *Pastoral*, pp. 70–1.

4 See Bornkamm, ibid. and H. W. Beyer, art. *episkopos*, *TDNT*, ii, pp. 608–22.

5 Barrett, *Pastoral*, p. 129.

6 Bornkamm, *TDNT*, vi, p. 667; Hanson, *Pastoral*, pp. 40–1, 111; B. H. Streeter, *The Primitive Church* (London 1929), pp. 108 f; H. von Campenhausen, *Ecclesiastical Authority and Spiritual Power in the Church of the First Three Centuries* (London 1969), pp. 107–8.

7 Bornkamm, *TDNT*, vi, p. 663.

8 von Campenhausen, *Authority*, p. 81.

9 M. Goguel, *The Primitive Church* (London 1963), p. 137.

10 E. Schweizer, *Church Order in the New Testament* (London 1961), p. 74 n. 283.

11 E.g., Barrett, *Pastoral*, p. 81; Kelly, *Pastoral*, pp. 127–8.

12 E.g., Dibelius-Conzelmann, *Pastoral*, p. 80; Hanson, *Pastoral*, p. 63.

13 Barrett, *Luke*, p. 73 n. 84.

14 E. Schweizer, *Order*, p. 72.

15 For this and the following paragraph see von Campenhausen, *Authority*, pp. 112–18.

16 von Campenhausen, *Authority*, p. 155.

17 E. Käsemann, *Essays on New Testament Themes* (London 1964), pp. 136–48.

18 Barrett, *Luke*, p. 75.

19 Schweizer, *Order*, p. 80.

20 von Campenhausen, *Authority*, p. 132.

21 Schweizer, *Order*, p. 78.

22 von Campenhausen, *Authority*, pp. 111–12.

CHAPTER 7 CHRISTOLOGY

1 See the recent works by F. Hahn, *The Titles of Jesus in Christology* (London 1969) and R. H. Fuller, *The Foundations of New Testament Christology* (London 1969).

2 Conzelmann, *Theology*, pp. 170–1.

3 C. H. Talbert, *Literary Patterns, Theological Themes and the Genre of Luke–Acts* (Missoula 1974), pp. 111–12.

4 Wilckens, *Missionsreden*, p. 156.

5 G. W. H. Lampe, 'The Lucan Portrait of Christ', *NTS*, 2 (1956), 160–75, here 167.

6 J. G. Davies, 'The Prefigurement of the Ascension in the Third Gospel', *JTS*, n.s. 6 (1955), 230; Conzelmann, *Theology*, p. 195; Talbert, *Patterns*, pp. 114–15.

7 Conzelmann, *Theology*, pp. 195 f.

8 C. F. Evans, *Resurrection and the New Testament* (London 1970), p. 96; Franklin, *Christ*, pp. 30–1.

9 See further in Wilson, *Gentiles*, pp. 96–107; Franklin, *Christ*, pp. 29 f; Talbert, *Patterns*, pp. 112–16.

10 Talbert, *Patterns*, p. 112.

11 Wilson, *Gentiles*, p. 106.

12 Franklin, *Christ*, pp. 40–1.

13 Esp. Wilckens, *Missionsreden*, pp. 137–56; H. Braun, 'Zur Terminologie der Acta von der Auferstehung Jesu', *TLZ*, 77 (1952), 533–6.

14 A. N. Wilder, 'Variant Traditions of the Resurrection in Acts', *JBL*, 62 (1943), 313–18; Talbert, *Patterns*, p. 112; Franklin, *Christ*, pp. 32–3.

15 Wilckens, *Missionsreden*, p. 150; H. Conzelmann, *Die Apostelgeschichte* (Tübingen 1963), p. 30.

16 C. F. D. Moule, 'The Christology of Acts', *SLA*, pp. 159–85, here pp. 160–1; followed by R. Longenecker, *The Christology of Early Jewish Christianity* (Nashville 1971), pp. 67–8.

17 Franklin, *Christ*, p. 50–3.

18 Hahn, *Christology*, p. 82.

19 Hahn, *Christology*, pp. 89 f; Fuller, *Christology*, pp. 156 f.

20 H. J. Cadbury, *BC*, v, p. 358.

21 Moule, 'Christology', p. 175; Longenecker, *Christology*, p. 174–5.

22 Fuller, *Christology*, p. 159; Hahn, *Christology*, pp. 159–60.

23 Franklin, *Christ*, pp. 55–7.

24 Hahn, *Christology*, pp. 161–8; Fuller, *Christology*, pp. 158–9.

25 Conzelmann, *Theology*, p. 171.

26 In general see W. Foerster and G. Fohrer, art. *sozo*, *TDNT*, vii, pp. 965 f; Marshall, *Luke*, thinks salvation is the key concept in Luke–Acts.

27 Haenchen, *Acts*, p. 206; Conzelmann, *Apg.*, p. 33; Wilckens, *Missionsreden*, pp. 175–6. Contrast Cadbury, *BC*, v, p. 370.

28 Hahn, *Christology*, pp. 305–6.

29 Wilckens, *Missionsreden*, p. 177.

30 E. Schweizer, 'The Concept of the Davidic Son of God in Acts and its Old Testament Background', *SLA*, pp. 186–93, here p. 187 f.

31 Hahn, *Christology*, pp. 265–88. R. Zehnle, *Peter's Pentecost Discourse* (Nashville 1971), pp. 47 f argues at length for a Moses typology in Acts 3 and 7.

32 Wilckens, *Missionsreden*, pp. 163 f; Moule, 'Christology', p. 169.

33 Moule, 'Christology', pp. 169–70; Franklin, *Christ*, pp. 61 f; J. Jeremias, art. *pais theou*, *TDNT*, v, pp. 704 f.

34 Hahn, *Christology*, pp. 375–6; Zehnle, *Pentecost*, pp. 48–9.

35 Though not to the degree Wilckens (*Missionsreden*, pp. 169–70) supposes.

36 Jeremias, *TDNT*, v, p. 707.

37 C. H. Talbert, 'The Concept of Immortals in Mediterranean Antiquity', *JBL*, 94 (1975), 419–36, esp. 435.

38 See further Moule, 'Christology', pp. 179 f; Lampe, 'Portrait', 174 f; Conzelmann, *Theology*, pp. 176 f; Marshall, *Luke*, pp. 179 f.

39 Conzelmann, *Theology*, pp. 173–84; Wilckens, *Missionsreden*, pp. 137–9, 151–2.

40 Talbert, *Patterns*, pp. 111 f.

41 Wilckens, *Missionsreden*, pp. 153 f, 234–5; Fuller, *Christology*, pp. 159 f; Hahn, *Christology*, pp. 164 f. Cf. J. A. T. Robinson, 'The Most Primitive Christology of All?', *JTS*, n.s. 7 (1956), 177–88, whose view is discussed by Moule, 'Christology', pp. 167–9; J. C. O'Neill, *The Acts of the Apostles in its Historical Setting* (1st edn, London 1961), pp. 124–9; Longenecker, *Christology*, pp. 77 f.

42 O. Bauernfeind, *Die Apostelgeschichte* (Leipzig 1939), pp. 66 f; Wilckens, *Missionsreden*, pp. 171 f.

43 *Contra* Haenchen, *Acts*, pp. 210–12; Conzelmann, *Apg.*, pp. 33–4; G. Lohfink, 'Christologie und Geschichtsbild in Apg. 3.19–21', *BZ*, 13 (1969), 223–41.

44 See above, p. 75.

45 Haenchen, *Acts*, p. 187; Fuller, *Christology*, pp. 184 ff; Hahn, *Christology*, pp. 106 f.

46 Wilckens, *Missionsreden*, pp. 171–5, 237–9; Conzelmann, *Apg.*, p. 30.

47 Zehnle, *Pentecost*, p. 70; O'Neill, *Acts*, 1st edn, pp. 126–7; Franklin, *Christ*, pp. 56–7.

48 H. Windisch, 'Zur Christologie der Pastoralbriefe', *ZNW*, 34 (1935), 213–38. Cf. Dibelius-Conzelmann, *Pastoral*, pp. 4, 9–10; Brox, *Pastoralbriefe*, pp. 162–5; Spicq, *Pastorales*, pp. 245–51.

49 W. Foerster, art. *soteria*, *TDNT*, vii, pp. 1016 f.

50 J. A. Allen, 'The "In Christ" Formula in the Pastoral Epistles', *NTS*, 10 (1963–4), 115–20.

51 Dibelius-Conzelmann, *Pastoral*, p. 42.

52 Barrett, *Pastoral*, p. 51; Brox, *Pastoralbriefe*, pp. 127–8.

53 Dibelius-Conzelmann, *Pastoral*, p. 9.

54 On Rom. 1.3 f see commentaries ad. loc.; Hahn, *Christology*, pp. 246 f; Fuller, *Christology*, pp. 165 f; M. Hengel, *The Son of God* (Philadelphia 1976), pp. 59 f; Windisch does not discuss the possibility of a pre-Pauline version.

55 Windisch, 'Christologie', 221.

56 Barrett, *Pastoral*, p. 25; Kelly, *Pastoral*, p. 54; Spicq, *Pastorales*, p. 344.

57 Barrett, *Pastoral*, p. 25; Easton, *Pastoral*, p. 41; Kelly, *Pastoral*, p. 163.

58 *Contra* Windisch, 'Christologie', 221–2.

59 Brox, *Pastoralbriefe*, p. 165.

60 Barrett, *Pastoral*, p. 65; Kelly, *Pastoral*, pp. 90 f; Brox, *Pastoralbriefe*, pp. 64, 160.

61 For a full discussion of the overall structure and the meaning of individual lines see R. H. Gundry, 'The Form, Meaning, and Background of the Hymn quoted in 1 Tim. 3.16', *Apostolic History and the Gospel* (Exeter 1970), ed. W. Ward Gasque and R. P. Martin, pp. 203–22.

62 Barrett, *Pastoral*, p. 138; Dibelius-Conzelmann, *Pastoral*, 143; Kelly, *Pastoral*, p. 246; Scott, *Pastoral*, p. 169; Brox, *Pastoralbriefe*, p. 300; Spicq, *Pastorales*, pp. 249, 640–1; Windisch, 'Christologie', 226–7.

63 Kelly, *Pastoral*, p. 246.

64 Both quotations from Dibelius-Conzelmann, *Pastoral*, p. 9.

CHAPTER 8 LAW AND SCRIPTURE

1 So, for example, Barrett, *Pastoral*, p. 43; Kelly, *Pastoral*, p. 48; Dibelius-Conzelmann, *Pastoral*, p. 21. On *nomodidaskalos* see Spicq, *Pastorales*, pp. 92 f.

2 Barrett, *Pastoral*, p. 53.

3 Bauer, p. 543; Liddell and Scott, 8th edn, p. 1008.

4 *Contra* Kelly, *Pastoral*, p. 49; J. Jeremias, *Die Briefe an Timotheus und Titus* (Göttingen 1963), p. 48.

5 Dibelius-Conzelmann, *Pastoral*, p. 22.

6 Moule, 'Problem', 432.

7 Scott, *Pastoral*, p. 11.

8 On the law in Luke–Acts see especially Conzelmann, *Theology*, pp. 158–61; Vielhauer, 'Paulinism', pp. 37–42; H. von Campenhausen, *The Formation of the Christian Bible* (Philadelphia 1972), pp. 37–50; and the intriguing and original essay by J. Jervell, *Luke and the People of God* (Minneapolis 1972), pp. 133–52.

9 Jervell, *Luke*, pp. 136–7.

10 Jervell, *Luke*, pp. 153 f.

11 Jervell, *Luke*, pp. 174–7.

12 J. C. O'Neill, *Acts*, 2nd edn, pp. 113 f.

13 von Campenhausen, *Formation*, p. 44; Haenchen, *Acts*, pp. 450 n. 1, 459.

14 M. Dibelius, *Studies in the Acts of the Apostles* (London 1956), p. 97.

15 W. Schmithals, *Paul and James* (London 1965), p. 100. O'Neill, *Acts*, 2nd edn, p. 111, correctly rejects Schmithal's view that the prohibition of 'what is strangled and blood' might be related to pagan accusations that Christians murdered and ate children.

16 Haenchen, *Acts*, p. 694.

17 Commentaries, ad loc.

18 This identification is much clearer in Titus than in Acts. On the complicated problem of the origin of the second quotation in Acts 17.28 compare F. F. Bruce, *The Acts of the Apostles* (Aberdeen 1951), p. 338, and Haenchen, *Acts*, pp. 524–5.

19 *Contra* Scott, *Pastoral*, p. 127.

20 Moule, 'Problem', 444; Strobel, 'Schreiben', 202.

21 See further Conzelmann, *Theology*, pp. 157–62; von Campenhausen, *Formation*, pp. 47–50; M. Rese, *Alttestamentliche Motive in der Christologie des Lukas* (Gütersloh 1969).

22 Jervell, *Luke*, esp. pp. 174–7, but all the chapters are relevant. Wilson, *Gentiles*, pp. 219–38. I think it improbable that the problem of the Lucan churches was a wholly internal one, a spontaneous identity crisis unrelated to Jewish or Jewish Christian pressures— see K. Löning, *Die Saulustradition in der Apostelgeschichte* (Münster 1973), p. 192.

23 Jervell, ibid., seems unsure.

24 H. Koester suggests a similar, 'daring interpretation of Scripture' by
    gnostics in Rev. 2.14–20: 'GNOMAI DIAPHOROI: The Origin
    and Nature of Diversification in Early Christianity', *Trajectories
    through Early Christianity*, ed. J. M. Robinson and H. Koester
    (Philadelphia 1971), pp. 114–57, esp. 148–9. For further discussion
    on the setting of Acts and the Pastorals see the next chapter.

CHAPTER 9   THE PORTRAIT OF PAUL

1   Brox, 'Lukas', 70.

2   G. Klein, *Die Zwölf Apostel* (Göttingen 1961), pp. 133–8, esp. p. 134.

3   G. Kittel, art. *blasphemia*, *TDNT*, i, pp. 621–5.

4   Dibelius-Conzelmann, *Pastoral*, p. 24; Haenchen, *Acts*, p. 410;
    Wilson, *Gentiles*, pp. 209–10.

5   Dibelius-Conzelmann, *Pastoral*, p. 28. It is perhaps more accurate to
    say that it is 'unlikely' rather than 'inconceivable'.

6   Barrett, *Pastoral*, p. 45.

7   *Contra* Klein, *Apostel*, pp. 114–44; see Wilson, *Gentiles*, pp. 157–9.

8   If Luke was the author of the Pastorals, he may have believed that
    Timothy was left behind after Paul's farewell speech and that
    2 Timothy was composed during the Roman imprisonment of Acts
    28. See the next chapter.

9   2 Tim. 4.11 is not necessarily contradicted by 2 Tim. 4.21, since in
    the former passage he is speaking of his close companions who had
    regularly accompanied him on his missionary tours and in the latter
    of local Christians who could give him moral support but who could
    not replace close friends.

10 Brox, *Pastoralbriefe*, p. 276.

11 Kelly, *Pastoral*, p. 178; Jeremias, *Timotheus*, p. 48.

12 Dibelius-Conzelmann, *Pastoral*, pp. 108–9; Brox, *Pastoralbriefe*,
    p. 243.

13 C. K. Barrett, 'Pauline Controversies in the post-Pauline Period',
    NTS, 20 (1973–4), 229–45, here 240.

14 C. H. Talbert, *Luke and the Gnostics* (New York 1966), pp. 71–82.
    Cf. W. Lutgert, *Die Irrlehrer der Pastoralbriefe*, (Gütersloh 1909),
    pp. 73 f.

15 Brox, *Pastoralbriefe*, pp. 68–74.

16 Wilson, *Gentiles*, pp. 116 f. See also J. Roloff, *Apostolat–Verkundig-
    ung–Kirche* (Gütersloh 1965).

17 J. Andrew Kirk, 'Apostleship since Rengstorf: Towards a Synthesis',
    NTS, 21 (1974–5), 249–64, here 264.

18 Wilson, *Gentiles*, p. 117.

19 Klein, *Apostle*, pp. 162–84.

20 Wilson, *Gentiles*, pp. 173 f.

21 See the formative article by J. Munck, 'Discours d'adieu dans le Nouveau Testament et dans la littérature biblique', *Aux sources de la tradition chrétienne* (Neuchâtel 1950), pp. 115 f.

22 Talbert, *Luke*, pp. 65–8, 114; Brox, *Pastoralbriefe*, pp. 72–3; von Campenhausen, *Authority*, pp. 111–12; J. Dupont, *Le Discours de Milet* (Paris 1962) has an extensive discussion of Acts 20.18 f.

23 Haenchen, *Acts*, p. 593. See below p. 121.

24 Haenchen, *Acts*, pp. 596–7.

25 Klein, *Apostel*, pp. 183–4.

26 W. Schmithals, *The Office of the Apostle in the Early Church* (Nashville 1969), p. 249.

27 Brox, *Pastoralbriefe*, pp. 72–4.

28 Talbert, *Luke*, p. 114.

29 Strobel, *Schreiben*, 203–5.

30 Brox, 'Lukas', 71.

31 Moule, 'Problem', 434.

32 For a general exploration of Pauline tradition, see Barrett, 'Controversies', 229–45; H. M. Schrenke, 'Das Weiterwirken des Paulus und die Pflege seines Erbes durch die Paulus-Schule', *NTS*, 21 (1974–5), 505–18.

33 Brox, *Pastoralbriefe*, pp. 66–77. See also Dibelius-Conzelmann, *Pastoral*, pp. 65 f; Spicq, *Pastorales*, pp. 85–119; and for a different view R. J. Karris, 'The Background and Significance of the Polemic of the Pastoral Epistles', *JBL*, 92 (1973), 549–64.

34 Compare Barrett, *Pastoral*, pp. 14–17.

35 E.g., Klein, *Apostel*, p. 181; Haenchen, *Acts*, p. 593; Talbert, *Patterns*, pp. 101–3.

36 Barrett, 'Controversies', 241.

CHAPTER 10 PAULINE CHRONOLOGY

1 Haenchen, *Acts*, p. 581; Barrett, *Pastoral*, p. 8.

2 The Apollos of Tit. 3.13 may not be the same as the Apollos of Acts 18.24—19.1; 1 Cor. 1.12; 3.4, 22; 4.6; 16.12.

3 Harrison, *Problem*, pp. 115–18.

4 See above p. 113.

5 Dibelius-Conzelmann, *Pastoral*, p. 125.

6 Easton, *Pastoral*, pp. 75–7. He also suggests that 4.19–22 may be author's addition or that the whole passage may be fictitious. Dibelius-Conzelmann, *Pastoral*, pp. 124–7, argue for a Caesarean

setting for 4.9–22 and for the whole of 2 Timothy. But 2 Tim. 1.17 flatly contradicts this. Harrison, *Problem*, pp. 118 f, thinks 2 Tim. 4.9–22 contains genuine material, but goes through the unnecesssarily complex procedure of dividing it into four separate notes.

7 Eusebius, *Hist. Eccl.*, ii, 22, 203; Jerome, *De vir. illust.*, 5; Chrysostom, *2 Tim. Hom.*, 2–3. For a recent revival of this hypothesis see W. Metzger, *Die letzte Reise des Apostels Paulus* (Stuttgart 1976).

8 Acts of Peter is found at the beginning of the Latin MS *Actus Vercellenses*; see E. Hennecke, *New Testament Apocrypha* (London 1965), vol. ii, pp. 270–82. For Muratorian Canon see Hennecke, *Apocrypha*, vol. i, pp. 43–4.

9 K. Lake, *BC*, i, pp. 326 f.

10 Haenchen, *Acts*, pp. 724–6.

11 Kelly, *Pastoral*, p. 198.

CHAPTER 11 CONCLUSION

1 See above pp. 118 f.

2 E.g. Brox refuses (justifiably) to be persuaded by Strobel's brief comparison of the theology of Luke and the Pastorals: Brox, 'Lukas', 67 f.

3 E.g. A. Plummer, *St Luke* (Edinburgh 1910), lviii–lix; H. W. Montefiore, *A Commentary on the Epistle to the Hebrews* (London 1964), p. 1.

4 E.g. E. M. Sidebottom, *James, Jude and 2 Peter* (London 1967), pp. 97–8.

5 Especially H. von Campenhausen, 'Polykarp von Smyrna und die Pastoralbriefe', in *Aus der Frühzeit des Christentums* (Tübingen 1963), pp. 197–252.

6 K. Stendhal, *The School of St Matthew* (Philadelphia 1968).

7 A. Culpepper, *The Johannine School* (Missoula 1975) is an excellent discussion. He rightly insists on a careful definition of the term 'school'.

8 H. Conzelmann, 'Luke's Place in the Development of Early Christianity', *SLA*, pp. 298–316, here pp. 307 f.

9 See Chapter 1 above.

10 Haenchen, *Acts*, pp. 86–7. Concerning Luke's access to traditions about Paul see C. Burchard, 'Paulus in der Apostelgeschichte', *TLZ*, 100 (1975), 881–95, and the literature cited there.

11 J. Quinn, 'P⁴⁶—The Pauline Canon?', *CBQ*, 36 (1974), 379–85, here 385 n. 36, suggests that Luke 'edited' the Pastorals and that they were published as the third volume of Luke–Acts. See also his

forthcoming essay, 'The last volume of Luke, the relation of Luke–Acts to the Pastoral Epistles', in *Perspectives on Luke–Acts*, ed. C. H. Talbert. 1978.

12 Some identify the two groups—but see E. J. Fiorenza, 'Apocalyptic and Gnosis in the Book of Revelation', *JBL*, 92 (1973), 565–81, here 571–2.

13 Conzelmann, 'Development', p. 302.

14 G. D. Kilpatrick, 'A Jewish Background to Acts 2.9–11?', *Journal of Jewish Studies*, 26 (1975), 48–9.

15 V. J. Robbins, 'By Land and By Sea: A Study in Acts 13—28', *SBL Seminar Papers*, 1976, pp. 381–96, esp. p. 394.

16 Conzelmann, 'Development', pp. 308–9; Windisch, 'Christologie', 233 f.

17 E. J. Goodspeed, *New Solutions to New Testament Problems* (Chicago 1927).

18 Moule, 'Problem', 452.

19 C. H. Talbert, 'The Book of Acts', *Review and Expositor*, lxxi (1974), 437–49, here 442–3; Schmithals, *Apostle*, pp. 258 f.

Index of Subjects

Index of Modern Authors

Index of Main Scriptural
Passages Discussed

161